Air Force

Wisconsin/Warner Bros. Screenplay Series

Air Force

Edited with an introduction by

Lawrence Howard Suid

Published for the Wisconsin Center for Film and Theater Research by
The University of Wisconsin Press

Published 1983

The University of Wisconsin Press
114 North Murray Street
Madison, Wisconsin 53715

The University of Wisconsin Press, Ltd.
1 Gower Street
London WC1E 6HA, England

First printing

Printed in the United States of America

Library of Congress Cataloging in Publication Data
Nichols, Dudley, 1895–
Air Force.
(Wisconsin/Warner Bros. screenplay series)
Includes bibliographical references.
I. Suid, Lawrence H.
II. Wisconsin Center for Film and Theater Research.
III. Title. IV. Series.
PN1997.A3145 1982 791.43'72 81-70290
ISBN 0-299-09000-0 AACR2
ISBN 0-299-09004-3 (pbk.)

Contents

Foreword 7
Tino Balio

Introduction: Mythmaking for the War Effort 9
Lawrence Howard Suid

Illustrations 35

Air Force 49

Notes to the Screenplay 220

Production Credits 222

Cast 223

Inventory 224

Foreword

In donating the Warner Film Library to the Wisconsin Center for Film and Theater Research in 1969, along with the RKO and Monogram film libraries and UA corporate records, United Artists created a truly great resource for the study of American film. Acquired by United Artists in 1957, during a period when the major studios sold off their films for use on television, the Warner library is by far the richest portion of the gift, containing eight hundred sound features, fifteen hundred short subjects, nineteen thousand still negatives, legal files, and press books, in addition to screenplays for the bulk of the Warner Brothers product from 1930 to 1950. For the purposes of this project, the company has granted the Center whatever publication rights it holds to the Warner films. In so doing, UA has provided the Center another opportunity to advance the cause of film scholarship.

Our goal in publishing these Warner Brothers screenplays is to explicate the art of screenwriting during the thirties and forties, the so-called Golden Age of Hollywood. In preparing a critical introduction and annotating the screenplay, the editor of each volume is asked to cover such topics as the development of the screenplay from its source in the final shooting script, differences between the final shooting script and the release print, production information, exploitation and critical reception of the film, its historical importance, its directorial style, and its position within the genre. He is also encouraged to go beyond these guidelines to incorporate supplemental information concerning the studio system of motion picture production.

We could set such an ambitious goal because of the richness of the script files in the Warner Film Library. For many film titles, the files might contain the property (novel, play, short story, or original story idea), research materials, variant drafts of scripts (from story outline to treatment to shooting script), post-production items such as press books and dialogue continuities, and legal records (details of the acquisition of the property, copyright registration, and contracts with actors and directors). Editors of the Wisconsin/Warner Bros. Screenplay Series receive copies of all the materials, along with prints of the films (the most authoritative ones available for reference purposes), to use in preparing the introductions and annotating the final shooting scripts.

In the process of preparing the screenplays for publication, typographical errors were corrected, punctuation and capitalization were modernized, and the format was redesigned to facilitate readability.

Unless otherwise specified, the photographs are frame enlargements taken from a 35-mm print of the film provided by United Artists.

In 1977 Warner Brothers donated the company's production records and distribution records to the University of Southern California and Princeton University, respectively. These materials are now available to researchers and complement the contents of the Warner Film Library donated to the Center by United Artists.

Tino Balio
General Editor

Introduction
Mythmaking for the War Effort

Lawrence Howard Suid

Most Americans remember World War II as the last good war, a popular conflict fought out of necessity, with evil going down to defeat. In postwar years, the film industry reinforced this image in countless war movies made with assistance from the armed forces. The relationship between Hollywood and the military had its origins before World War I. By the end of the 1920s, the process by which the armed forces extended cooperation to filmmakers had become formalized as a result of the help given to such combat movies as *The Big Parade* (1925), *What Price Glory* (1926), and *Wings* (1927). During the 1930s, Hollywood used the peacetime military mostly as a setting for song and dance musicals and comedies designed as escapist entertainment to take American minds off the nation's economic troubles.

By the end of the 1930s, as Germany and Japan began to pose threats to the United States, Hollywood returned to serious movies about the military, portraying the services preparing to defend the nation against possible attack. Such films as *Flight Command* (1940), *I Wanted Wings* (1941), and *Dive Bomber* (1941) showed the American people how the Navy and Army Air Corps trained for their anticipated missions. From the film industry's point of view, these pseudodocumentary movies enabled studios to put popular actors into military settings where the filmmakers could combine visually exciting flying sequences with the obligatory romantic interludes.

On their part, the armed services believed the movies provided them informational and recruiting value. Whether they accomplished the expected mission remains open to debate. One viewer wrote to Secretary of Navy Frank Knox on December 1, 1941, saying, "If there ever was a picture shown to discourage anyone from joining the Air Corps it is the picture *Dive Bomber*." The writer thought it would lead every "potential draftee to stay clear of aviation" because the film showed that "every aviator loses his health due to flying. Perhaps this is so, but it seems a queer time to advertise this throughout the country. If this picture was made in Germany and sent here I could see the point." Although recognizing that the film was intended to educate the public, he observed that it "sure won't get any recruits in the air service."[1] In response to a similar letter, the Navy's public relations office said that the general reaction to the film had been favorable and suggested that if the movie had shown only the positive side of the aviation story, "it would not ring true and would be declared propaganda by the public."[2]

Charles Lindbergh and other isolationists throughout the country were labeling *Dive Bomber* and more than a dozen other recent Hollywood releases just that. On September 11, in Des Moines, Iowa, the Lone Eagle told an America First rally: "The three most important groups pressing the country toward war are the British, the Jewish and the Roosevelt administration." To Lindbergh, the Jews were particularly dangerous because of "their large ownership and influence in our motion pictures, our press, our radio and our Government."[3]

Concidentally with Lindbergh's crusade, isolationists in the United States Senate were orchestrating an investigation of the film industry and its supposed pro-Allied sympathies. Senators Burton K. Wheeler (Dem., Montana), Gerald P. Nye (Rep., North Dakota), D. Worth Clark (Dem., Idaho), and Bennett Champ Clark (Dem., Missouri) led the attack, accusing Hollywood of persistently making movies calculated to drag the

1. Arthur Keil to Frank Knox, December 1, 1941, Record Group 80, Box 94, National Archives, Washington, D.C.

2. Lt. Alan Brown to E. C. Roworth, August 26, 1941, Record Group 80, Box 94, National Archives, Washington, D.C.

3. *New York Times*, September 12, 1941.

United States into the European war. In hearings before a subcommittee of the Committee on Interstate Commerce convened on September 9, film executives—with Wendell Willkie, the unsuccessful 1940 Republican Presidential candidate, as their counsel—denied the charges, arguing that the industry made movies purely for entertainment and profit.

Harry Warner, president of Warner Brothers, for one, acknowledged he was "opposed to nazi-ism" and told the subcommittee, "I abhor and detest every principle and practice of the Nazi movement. To me, nazi-ism typifies the very opposite of the kind of life every decent man, woman, and child wants to live." He denied that the pictures produced by his company were "propaganda" as the senators had alleged. Rejecting Senator Nye's claim that *Sergeant York* was designed to create war hysteria, Warner maintained that the film "is a factual portrait of the life of one of the great heroes of the last war. If that is propaganda, we plead guilty." Likewise, the studio head said, *Confessions of a Nazi Spy* (1939) was a "factual portrayal of a Nazi spy ring that actually operated in New York City. If that is propaganda, we plead guilty." In fact, Warner argued, these films were "carefully prepared on the basis of factual happenings and they were not twisted to serve any ulterior purpose." Most important, he said that "millions of average citizens have paid to see these pictures. They have enjoyed wide popularity and have been profitable to our company. In short, these pictures have been judged by the public and the judgment has been favorable." While acknowledging that his company regularly made feature films about the military, he stressed that the studio "needed no urging from the Government and we would be ashamed if the Government would have to make such requests of us. We have produced these pictures voluntarily and proudly."[4]

Ultimately, the hearings did little more than produce acrimonious exchanges between the senators and film executives, and they were recessed until mid-December. Probably the only

4. U.S. Congress, Senate, *Propaganda in Motion Pictures: Hearings before a Subcommittee of the Committee on Interstate Commerce*, 77th Cong., 1st sess., September 9–26, 1941, pp. 338–40.

demonstratable impact the cited films had was that the isolationists' reaction to them led to the convening of the hearings. In any event, Pearl Harbor rendered the debate over American participation in the war moot and opened the floodgates for the production of movies about the American experience in World War II. The first films to reach the screen after Pearl Harbor—*To the Shores of Tripoli, Flying Tigers*, and *Across the Pacific*—had been in production before December 7. For the most part, their studios simply added appropriate tag lines to the stories to reflect the United States' entry into the war and to advocate the need for everyone to support the budding war effort.

To the Shores of Tripoli focused on training at the Marine Corps' recruit depot in San Diego. Since the film was already in production before December 7, it had only a tangential connection to the early months of the war. In fact, a second unit had gone to Hawaii to film scheduled battle maneuvers and had done shooting in Pearl Harbor the day before the Japanese attack. While the footage of target practice at sea provided a visual spectacle for audiences, actual combat footage of Pacific battles shown in theaters before the release of *To the Shores of Tripoli* in April made the training maneuvers in the film obsolete and lacking in drama. Nevertheless, in approving the movie for distribution, the Navy Department wrote to Darryl Zanuck, head of production at 20th Century-Fox, that "the reaction to the picture was excellent" and indicated that "much mutual benefit will be derived from the showing of this picture."[5]

The Flying Tigers, which also focused on the period before Pearl Harbor, served as a tribute to the volunteer American fliers who fought the Japanese in China before the United States entered the war. The film related the perennial story of a stereotypical squadron commander, played by John Wayne, who must deal with a disparate group of men, each trying to fight the overwhelming Japanese enemy in his own way. According to *Time* magazine, Wayne was "a rudimentary actor, but he has the look and bearing, unusual in his trade, of a capable human

5. Record Group 80, Box 94, National Archives.

male. As the squadron commander, he is able to make his habitual inarticulateness suggest the uncommunicative competence that men expect in their leaders."[6]

David Miller, who had finished shooting the film before Pearl Harbor, acknowledged that *The Flying Tigers* had two purposes: to entertain and to warn the nation about its potential enemies. The director said that Hollywood rarely made movies "to boost the morale of the Americans." Nevertheless, 1941 was a time of crisis in the director's mind: "My gosh, America was preparing and actually fighting. Anything to boost the morale of the country . . . so that factories could work longer, so that people would go into defense industries." Personally, Miller thought the United States should have gotten into the war sooner, but said he didn't make *The Flying Tigers* "to reflect that emotion onto the American public." He admitted, however, that "making a film to stir up the people and make them realize who the enemy is and what the enemy was doing and what the enemy could accomplish were always coupled in my mind with the threat of the Nazi regime. In fact, when Japan signed a pact with Hitler, [it] became part of the Nazi regime as far as I was concerned."[7]

While both *To the Shores of Tripoli* and *The Flying Tigers* had bases in the realities of military life and historical events, John Huston's *Across the Pacific* offered viewers a typical Hollywood espionage-counterespionage thriller with the story created wholly in the filmmakers' minds. Humphrey Bogart, as an Army officer masquerading as a traitor, works to thwart Japanese agents trying to destroy the Panama Canal just before Pearl Harbor. In the end, as with all good melodramas, Bogart foils the plot and wins the girl. By the time *Across the Pacific* appeared in September, the Doolittle raid on Japan and the great victory at Midway had gone a long way to lifting the gloom that Pearl Harbor cast. Nevertheless, Bogart's melodramatic routing of the enemy with a blazing machine gun provided audiences a patriotic stimulus.

6. *Time*, October 12, 1942, p. 96.

7. Interview with David Miller, August 4, 1975.

Whatever their effect on morale, these films only served to provide Hollywood time for starting production on a series of original stories based on events of the first months of the war. While the resulting movies were intended to return a profit, filmmakers consciously designed their stories to stimulate the nation's patriotism and so the war effort.

Wake Island, the first production to be released after December 7, portrayed the Marines' desperate and ultimately doomed defense of Wake Island in December 1941. From a first-hand account of the only Marine to leave the island and some imaginative screenwriting, Paramount re-created the battle on the shore of the Salton Sea in California, using miniatures, special effects, and minimal Marine Corps cooperation. The *New York Times* reviewer thought that the story of Leathernecks' fighting to the last man would "surely bring a surge of pride to every patriot's breast" (September 2, 1941). Nevertheless, while successfully combining wartime action and propaganda, *Wake Island* lacked the scope and impact to portray the epic nature of the growing conflict. It remained for Warner Brothers' initial wartime production to capture the essence of the American combat experience in the early months of the war.

Planning the Production

Air Force had its inception with Jack Warner's desire to make a film about the Air Force. Immediately after Pearl Harbor, Warner, the studio's executive producer, inquired of General Hap Arnold, commanding officer of the Army Air Forces, as to the service's interest in such a project. On his part, Arnold had recognized the informational value of motion pictures ever since he had flown his Army biplane in the 1911 movie *Military Scout*. After briefly flirting with the idea of becoming an actor, Arnold had continued his military career but maintained ties with the film community as he rose through the ranks.[8]

While Arnold expressed enthusiasm for Warner's proposed film, he could promise the studio little cooperation, given the

8. Interview with Col. Bruce Arnold, March 19, 1977; *New York Times*, January 24, 1943; *Daily Variety*, February 3, 1943.

desperate military situation in the first months of the war. With Arnold's approval, however, the War Department put at the studio's disposal records and files relating to the air war, including actual statements from Air Force fliers for use by Dudley Nichols, whom Warner had assigned to write the screenplay.[9]

In early April, the Air Force appointed then Captain Samuel Triffy as a technical adviser to assist on the production. Triffy, who had worked on two *March of Time* productions as an Air Force adviser, had expected to go to the Far East as a bomber pilot. Instead, he found himself at Warner Brothers with orders to read a story to see if it could be made into a movie acceptable to the Air Force. After spending his first session at the studio simply talking with Jack Warner, producer Hal Wallis, and director Howard Hawks, Triffy asked to read the story. Hawks "smirked" and admitted the studio did not as yet have a story. The director told Triffy that the studio wanted him to help Nichols come up with an acceptable script.[10]

Although the armed forces have never included scriptwriting in their orders to technical advisers, officers assigned to work on military films have often provided uncredited assistance to screenwriters. Their help can range from simply providing correct flying dialogue, as the Navy's technical adviser did on *Bridges at Toko Ri*, to reshaping the entire production from a serious submarine story to a comedy, as the adviser did on *Operation Petticoat*. In Triffy's case, he spent eight weeks assisting Hawks and Nichols in developing a story and writing accurate dialogue.[11]

The entire process was complicated by Warner Brothers' desire to make and release the film as quickly as possible. All the surface water combat sequences were shot over an eight-week period on Santa Monica Bay before the script had advanced much beyond the talking stage. As reference point for scenes of

9. Interview with Col. Samuel Triffy, January 6, 1976. Information and quotations attributed to Triffy in the Introduction are also from that interview.

10. Triffy interview.

11. Triffy interview; interview with Capt. Marshall Beebe, technical adviser on *Bridges at Toko Ri*, March 20, 1974; interview with Adm. Lucius Chappell, technical adviser on *Operation Petticoat*, August 7, 1975.

mass destruction of a Japanese flotilla, the special effects department used the story of Lieutenant Colin Kelly's sinking of the Japanese battleship *Haruna* in the early days of fighting off the Philippines.[12] In fact, the original story had been a public relations creation intended to boost homefront morale following Pearl Harbor. While Kelly had died a hero's death, he had not sunk the battleship nor had American planes wreaked the havoc that Warner Brothers imaginatively manufactured. Moreover, by the time *Air Force* reached the screen in early 1943, reviewers and audiences assumed that the naval sequences represented the battle of Coral Sea or Midway,[13] even though the miniature shooting had been completed before the battles took place and the film's military action occurred in the Philippines.

In any event, in developing a coherent story, Nichols, Hawks, and Triffy had to keep in mind the special effects material already shot. Ultimately, the screenplay went through at least five drafts before Nichols completed the Revised Final shooting script dated July 3, 1942, with further changes dated October 8, 1942. Even that one served only as a framework. According to Triffy, Hawks created his film as he worked, changing the written dialogue during rehearsals to improve authenticity and drama. (The dialogue in the final shooting script, the Revised Final herein printed, bears only a general resemblance to the words the characters speak.)

By 1942, Hawks had gained this freedom and the control over every aspect of his films as a result of a reputation achieved during a Hollywood career that began as a writer in the early 1920s. After leaving Fox studio in 1929, Hawks never committed himself to a long-term contract, preferring to free-lance, often producing and contributing to the writing of the scripts in addition to directing. Although he became best known for action dramas, he directed such comedies as *Twentieth Century* (1934) and *His Girl Friday* (1940), detective melodramas, and gangster films, including the classic *Scarface* (1932). The success of these

12. Triffy interview.

13. *New York Daily Mirror*, February 4, 1943; *Weekly Variety*, February 3, 1943; *Time*, February 8, 1943, p. 85. The film does contain a small amount of combat footage, some of which was probably taken at the battle of Coral Sea or Midway.

movies and others, including *The Dawn Patrol* (1930), *Ceiling Zero* (1935), *Bringing up Baby* (1938), and *Sergeant York* (1941), gave the director the independence to stand up to Hollywood's most powerful executives. When Louis B. Mayer tried to dictate the casting on *Viva Villa!* (1934) at MGM, Hawks angrily confronted him, reinforced his goodbye with a violent shove, and walked out, vowing never to work for Mayer again. When he moved to Warner Brothers, he refused to work if Jack Warner came onto the set.[14]

For *Air Force,* Hawks started with Dudley Nichols's initial Temporary dated April 24, 1942, which told the story of a B-17 during the early days of the war. The writer devoted the screenplay's first fifty-five pages to developing the main characters and their personal relationships rather than focusing on the airplane and the actions of the Air Force following Pearl Harbor. The B-17, called the *Daisy Mae* in the first scripts, is one of a flight of heavy bombers that is sent to Hawaii on a training mission on December 6, 1941. Arriving at Pearl Harbor on the eve of the Japanese sneak attack, the *Daisy Mae* is quickly dispatched to the Philippines via Wake Island, both already under attack. Despite Triffy's assistance and pressure from the studio, Nichols's first script carried the *Daisy Mae* and her crew only as far as Clark Field. The last page ended: "And here we terminate Part IV for the time being. . . . And it is on this day that *Daisy Mae* goes out and sinks a battleship and is shot down in turn and we have real tragedy in the death of Kelly and the kid. And our story, which is already as long as the sky is wide (which shows how much it must be condensed), picks up speed and excitement and moves to a swift dramatic conclusion."

Believing the story should begin more effectively, Triffy went to Hal Wallis and reminded the producer that he and the Air Force had expected a documentary-style story about flying, not a Hollywood-style love story in a military setting. Wallis and Hawks apparently found the technical adviser's comments

14. See Bruce F. Kawin, ed., *To Have and Have Not* (Madison: University of Wisconsin Press, 1980), for a description of Hawks's making of that film. See also Robin Wood, *Howard Hawks* (Garden City, N.Y.: Doubleday, 1968).

valid, and by the time Nichols had completed the second draft of the script, dated May 29, the introductory character development and love interests had been severely condensed. Instead, the story began very much as it eventually did in the film, with the historical event, the flight of twelve B-17s leaving San Francisco for Pearl Harbor on the night of December 6. The new script developed the crew's personalities during preparations for departure and on the flight to Hawaii.

While the script was evolving, Warner Brothers faced the need to arrange for location shooting. Consequently, despite Triffy's objections to the story, in mid-May the studio sent the first 123 pages of the April 24 script, which ended with the *Daisy Mae* in Hawaii, and a five-page outline of the balance of the scenario to the War Department. In addition to carrying the story through the *Daisy Mae*'s arrival in the Philippines, which ended the first script, the outline blocked out the plane's subsequent war against Japan along the lines Hawks followed in the film.

In responding to Warners' accompanying request for cooperation, the Pictorial Branch of the War Department, on May 18, asked the Special Services Division for an "analysis as to military detail and advisability of giving full War Department cooperation on the filming of the picture. This is a special Air Corps recruiting job and I would appreciate the return of the script with your comments in twenty-four hours." Army Air Corps concurrence with the War Department's request was indicated in writing on the memo. In its answer the next day, Special Services wrote: "War Dept. approval and cooperation recommended."[15]

On its part, the War Department's Review Branch did recommend some changes in the military aspects of the script. In his comments, the branch chief asked why the screenplay stressed "our pre-war inadequacies," including the dialogue "All we've

15. Chief, Pictorial Branch, Bureau of Public Relations to Special Services Division, War Department, May 18, 1942; Special Services to Chief, Pictorial Branch, May 19, 1942, Record Group 165, Box 6, National Archives, hereafter cited as RG 165, NA.

got's side-arms!" He suggested that another portion of the script "could be rephrased to indicate American resourcefulness without overstressing our undefended position." On a security matter, the chief noted: "Mention of any blind spots of any aircraft or other indications of vulnerability is restricted. Also no reference may be made to position of turrets, cannon, and machine guns of Flying Fortresses."[16]

If the War Department had seen even two more pages of the initial script, its directive would undoubtedly have been even stronger. On page 125, Nichols had focused on one of the major deficiencies of the early models of the B-17, the lack of a tail gun emplacement. With the *Daisy Mae* back in the air on its way to Wake Island, one of the crew members mentions that the newer B-17E had "a stinger in her tail." Pointing up the vulnerability of their B-17D, a second member answers, "I sure wish *Daisy Mae* had one." In the final script and the completed film, reference to the redesigned B-17E disappeared. To improve the fighting ability of the star of the movie, however, the bomber's crew ultimately cuts the tail cone off the plane and inserts a machine gun, which provides the unsuspecting Japanese pilots a surprise during the climactic air battle.

By the time *Air Force* appeared in 1943, the issue had become moot because most of the B-17D's had been destroyed in the early fighting and those few that remained airworthy assumed noncombat roles. Moreover, both the Japanese and German pilots had already discovered the addition of machine guns to the tail of the B-17. In any event, since Triffy was acting as technical adviser during the scriptwriting and was joined during location shooting by Captain Hewitt Wheless, one of the early heroes of the air war in the Pacific, security matters would seldom become a problem for the filmmakers. Of real concern was finding equipment and a locale at which to shoot the exterior action.

Following notification of the War Department's script approval, Hal Wallis wrote back to Washington that the studio

16. Chief, Review Branch, to Chief, Pictorial Branch, May 19, 1942, RG 165, NA.

"will do everything possible to make it a really fine picture."[17] To facilitate this, Triffy returned to Washington in June to discuss the matter of available equipment and possible sites for location shooting. In a meeting, General Arnold lent his tacit approval to the project by giving Triffy a card on which he had written: "Good Idea. HHA." That was the technical adviser's only visible indication of Air Force support in obtaining needed material and permission for doing the flying sequences.[18]

Nevertheless, Triffy and Warner Brothers faced the reality that the Air Force was involved in more important matters than providing assistance to a film company. Moreover, the continuing fear of a Japanese invasion of the West Coast prevented the shooting anywhere near Hollywood of flying sequences in which planes would have to be decorated with Japanese markings. Consequently, Triffy flew to Florida to inspect sites and determine the availability of equipment and planes. After Triffy made a second trip to Florida with Hawks to inspect Drew Field near Tampa, the commanding officer of the base was informed that Warner Brothers wanted to do its location shooting there.[19] In a memo, the War Department said that it "desired that you extend such assistance as, in your judgment, is deemed necessary to insure the success of the sequences planned." It placed only one restriction on its cooperation: "It is the policy of the War Department not to allow soldiers or military equipment to be disguised and photographed as representing the personnel or equipment of foreign countries."[20]

Although this restriction, in one form or another, has been part of military regulations governing cooperation during both peace and war, local commanders have generally ignored its strictures. During the making of the 1927 Paramount classic *Wings*, half of the forty-five hundred men the Army lent to the

17. Chief, Pictorial Branch, War Department, to Jack L. Warner, May 19, 1942; Hal Wallis to Chief, Pictorial Branch, War Department, May 22, 1942, RG 165, NA.

18. Triffy interview.

19. Triffy interview.

20. Chief, Pictorial Branch, War Department, to Commanding Officer, Drew Field, June 6, 1942, RG 165, NA.

production during filming in Texas played German soldiers in the re-creation of the battle of Saint-Mihiel. American fighters and bombers also masqueraded as German planes during the many flying sequences. And, at about the same time that *Air Force* was being filmed in Florida, the Army was providing Columbia Pictures with five hundred American soldiers, trucks, and a fighter plane along the California-Arizona border to portray German men and equipment battling Humphrey Bogart in *Sahara*.

But if the War Department regulations themselves posed no real problem to Hawks and his film crew, Triffy still had to locate the necessary planes and arrange for them to be available when needed. According to the technical adviser, the Air Force could not "supply a hell of a lot of support for the film because everyone was concerned with the war." Operating alone, Triffy ultimately located the required aircraft and equipment through officers he knew who were in charge of military hardware in the Tampa area.

During the eight weeks the film company spent at Drew Field in late summer, Triffy flew both an Army two-place trainer and a fighter painted with the Rising Sun emblem in the combat sequences portraying Japanese attacks on American aircraft and military positions. In his stunt work, the technical adviser had to deal with a director more concerned with authentic-looking aerial action than with the safety of the planes or the pilot's life. According to Triffy, Hawks and the film company "were ruthless! Absolutely ruthless! If they could have damaged [an] airplane in flight so I would have had an accident, they would have done it. Really! I couldn't trust them. I mean it."[21]

Once, after completing an hour and a half's flying, Triffy discovered that his landing gear would not come down and he had to spend an hour doing a series of violent maneuvers before he could get the plane's wheels down and locked in place. Unaware of the problem, Hawks and the crew had gone to lunch.

21. General Wheless agreed with Triffy's observation but noted, "I think it was necessary in order to get the result they desired" (Wheless to Suid, June 23, 1977).

When the director returned to the field, he asked Triffy where he had been. After listening to the technical adviser's account, Hawks expressed his unhappiness that the film crew had not been notified of the malfunction so that it could have been prepared if Triffy had had to crash-land. The director told the flier, "We would have wanted that shot." Triffy responded, "And damage an airplane? You are out of your mind."

On his part, Hawks had only one goal: to make the movie using any means at his disposal, even if it meant making excessive demands on the Air Force. In his singlemindedness, the director continually strove to give *Air Force* a feeling of authenticity and believability. According to Triffy, Hawks "had an uncanny ability to obtain a freshness, a currentness, something that has more truth than fiction." To achieve this effect, the filmmaker discussed every scene and every item with the technical adviser and had his secretary take down everything. In each case, Triffy said, Hawks wanted to know what a real Air Force man would do and how he would feel while doing it.

In the process of putting the story on the screen, Dudley Nichols's several scripts provided Hawks with only the general framework in which to operate. In fact, only the Temporary script of April 24 and the Revised Final script of July 3 to October 8, 1942, carry Nichols's name. Given the way Hawks worked, it is possible to say only that the writer provided the original story and the characters. Even here, the final result received additional input from Hawks's friend and Warner Brothers' contract screenwriter William Faulkner to whom the director turned for help with two scenes.[22]

Along the way, the name of the movie's star underwent change. From *Daisy Mae* in the first two scripts, the plane became *Annie* in the Second Revised Temporary of June 12–13, 1942. By the next week, in the Final of June 18, 1942, *Annie* had become the *Mary Ann*, which it remained. Although in the historical event twelve B-17s flew from San Francisco, the *Mary Ann* is one of nine planes in the movie, perhaps because of the problem of acquiring use of twelve planes and precious gasoline during the first months of the war.

22. Kawin, *To Have and Have Not*, p. 32.

The actual lines the characters speak during the film evolved from collaboration between Hawks and Triffy, modifying Nichols's dialogue when necessary to assure authenticity of language. The technical adviser recalled, "The script was never shot, per se! . . . There was a thread of a story. That's all. He knew where he was going. But day to day, we didn't know. There were days when we didn't shoot one frame, not one frame . . . Howard and I talking or not talking or just thinking. It looked like nothing was going on, even from a negative standpoint."

When shooting did take place in Florida, Triffy orchestrated the flying sequences. To film the formation scenes of the B-17s on their way to Hawaii, he managed to collect nine of the four-engine bombers from bases in the Tampa area. In addition to piloting the single-engine planes masquerading as Japanese aircraft, Triffy flew the *Mary Ann* in the plane's solo sequences. After completing the location shooting, Triffy worked in Hollywood until early December, advising Hawks on all aspects of military procedures and language and developing a story line that would tie together the miniature sequences with the footage taken in Florida.

Among other tasks, Triffy supervised the building of mock-ups of the interior of a B-17 for shooting the interior scenes of the crew in flight. From General Dynamics, he obtained photographs and measurements to assure as much accuracy of detail as possible without jeopardizing military security. From Lockheed Aircraft, he acquired the cockpit control pedestal even though he had no formal military authorization. According to Triffy, Lockheed helped because it understood the purpose that the film would serve in the war effort.

In the end, Triffy was satisfied with the military authenticity and plausibility of the film. To be sure, as many directors of war films have done, Hawks took dramatic license in such matters as having a man hold a heavy machine gun in his hands and shoot down a strafing enemy fighter. Nevertheless, Triffy acknowledged that *Air Force* was "as authentic as we could make it under the circumstances. I was satisfied with that." He admitted, however, that he "was not really excited" about the completed film when he finally saw it after returning to active duty.

Triffy attributed his lukewarm reaction to having been "so intently involved with it." He was disappointed that the film did not do more to portray the feelings of fliers in war. Consequently, while he thought *Air Force* was a good film, he had "had more grandiose thoughts about what the finished product was going to be. Yet, it was good enough."

In fact, *Air Force* proved good enough to become the standard against which to measure all future World War II flying films. Combining Nichols's script and Triffy's military advice with his own style of directing, Hawks produced a classic action, adventure combat movie, gradually building to the climactic battle. Apart from an occasional clichéd line, the movie creates an ambience of men in war without the "authenticity" of four-letter words and vulgarities that filmmakers have come to equate with realism. Thanks to Triffy's insistence that Warner Brothers "not make a flying film about the war into a love story," *Air Force* contains very little nonmilitary business. Women appear only in a brief "family-parting" scene at the beginning of the movie and in a hospital sequence in Hawaii in the aftermath of the Pearl Harbor attack. Otherwise, Hawks relegates romance to the crew's bantering about their relationships with women.

The Story

Typical of all World War II movies, the crew comprises an ethnic and geographic cross section of the nation, except for a black. (Only Dore Schary ignored the reality of a segregated armed forces and cast a black as a soldier in *Bataan*. Despite the many critical letters he later received, Schary felt he had done the right thing.)[23] Despite its heterogeneous makeup, the crew includes the usual Hollywood stereotypes. The pilot, Captain Michael Quincannon (John Ridgely), is happily married with a wife who "will be waiting" for him. The copilot, Lieutenant Bill Williams (Gig Young), has a girl waiting for him to arrive in Hawaii. The girl is the sister of the bombardier, Lieutenant Tommy McMartin (Arthur Kennedy). The navigator, Lieutenant Monk Hauser (Charles Drake), tries to hide the fact that his father was a fa-

23. Interview with Dore Schary, December 20, 1973.

mous World War I pilot. The assistant crew chief, Corporal B. B. Weinberg (George Tobias), is a Jew from Brooklyn. The new aerial gunner, Sergeant Joe Winocki (John Garfield), is an embittered, washed-out pilot about to leave the service. The assistant radio operator, Private Henry Chester (Ray Montgomery), is the newest and youngest member of the crew. And the oldest member, the crew chief, Sergeant Robbie White (Harry Carey), serves as the plane's father figure and steadying force.

Air Force opens with a teletype machine printing out orders for a B-17 training mission from San Francisco to Hawaii. During the preflight briefing and preparation for the takeoff, the script briefly introduces the crew. Once the *Mary Ann* is in flight, Hawks effectively develops each man's character and, for dramatic purposes, the mandatory intracrew antagonisms. Quincannon had been one of Winocki's flight instructors and had recommended he be dismissed from pilot school. While the officer maintains his decision was correct, he tells Winocki early in the flight that gunners are an integral part of a plane: "Every man has got to rely on every other man to do the right thing at the right time."[24] Winocki will have none of it, revealing he is leaving the service in three weeks when his enlistment is up. The *Mary Ann* becomes airborne on the evening of December 6, 1941, as Lieutenant Hauser has written in his flight log.

Both in visual images of the formation above the calm sea and in words, Hawks creates a tranquil world as the planes head west. The crew discuss their homes, women, and anticipated pleasant stay in Hawaii. The radio carries the story of the forthcoming visit of Japan's "peaceful mission" to Washington. As the B-17s near Hawaii, however, the radio operator suddenly picks up snatches of frantic conversation, which Quincannon quickly recognizes as sounds of combat. From this point on, the *Mary Ann* becomes the center of attention and the real star of *Air Force*. The sneak attack, juxtaposed with the report of Japan's peace mission, also turns the film into a propaganda vehicle for conveying to the American people the message of Japanese duplicity, an image that Hawks quickly reinforces.

24. All dialogue is from the film rather than from the final shooting script herein printed.

Forced to divert to a small emergency landing field because of the continued bombing at Pearl Harbor, the *Mary Ann* suffers minor damage to a landing gear. While Sergeant White supervises temporary repairs, Lieutenants Williams and Hauser make contact with other planes from the formation that have landed at a second emergency airfield. On the way back, they run into some local Japanese whom the copilot later describes as "nice, friendly fellas." The apparent fifth columnists shoot at the men and trail them back to the *Mary Ann*. With the plane under attack, Quincannon manages to take off and land at Hickam Field at night, amidst the still-burning rubble of the attack.

There, the crew finds more Japanese sabotage. The colonel who greets the plane explains the destruction of a row of fighters: "Three vegetable trucks arrived from Honolulu this morning. When the first Jap plane showed up, the trucks went right down the field, smashed the tails off every ship on the land. Well, they sure had a field day! They took the first round, but there'll be others!" In fact, little if any damage on December 7 came from fifth columnists. Nevertheless, in 1943, when *Air Force* was released, the true story of Pearl Harbor was not yet widely known and audiences undoubtedly manifested the proper outrage.

Some people, who knew the truth, manifested "improper" outrage, however. In a speech on May 30, 1943, Socialist Norman Thomas observed that it was "especially regrettable that repeatedly and in detail the film falsely represents Japanese-Americans in Hawaii as guilty of acts of sabotage and violence against American forces. There is a legitimate propaganda use of movies, but falsehood is not legitimate in such propaganda, whether the theme is *Mission to Moscow* or the delicate subject of race relations." In response, Elmer Davis, head of the Office of War Information, wrote to Thomas that his office "endeavored to press upon the producers the unfortunate effects that might result from the very misrepresentations to which you object. Our efforts were not successful and . . . there was nothing more that we could do except to guard against repetition of the error by calling to the attention of all studios the findings of various investigators. We believe there will be no similar misrepresentations."[25]

Howard Hawks was not concerned with such matters, and he carefully reinforced the proper outrage as he developed the story. From the welcoming colonel, McMartin learns that his sister Susan (Faye Emerson) has been seriously wounded. At the hospital, McMartin and Williams meet Lieutenant Tex Rader (James Brown), a fighter pilot and Williams's rival for Susan's affection, who tells them what happened to Susan. Without explaining why they were together before 8 A.M., Rader says that he and Susan were trying to get back to his base. As they neared the field a delivery truck from Honolulu blocked the road. When he got out to investigate, Rader recalls, "The first thing I knew there was an explosion right in my face. There was a Jap behind the wheel with a shotgun. He was a rotten shot. I sloughed him over the head with his own gun and got the truck off the road." But when they reached the field, Rader says, Susan stood up in the car "yelling and rooting like she was at a football game" and was then machine-gunned by one of the attacking planes.

Williams and McMartin return to the field to find that the *Mary Ann* has received orders to fly on to the Philippines by way of Wake Island. The crew also finds it has a passenger, Lieutenant Rader. He is being sent to Manila as a replacement pilot, having shot down four Japanese planes before being knocked out of the sky. Apart from the dramatic tensions between Williams and Rader over their interest in McMartin's sister, Rader's presence aboard the *Mary Ann* gives the film the opportunity to argue the case for heavy bombers and bomber pilots against the glamour associated with fighter planes.

During the flight to Wake Island, the crew picks up on their shortwave radio President Roosevelt's war message to Congress with its prediction of "absolute victory" so that "treachery shall never again endanger us." The theme of Japanese "treachery" is

25. Norman Thomas speech, "The Economic Front"; Elmer Davis to Norman Thomas, May 31, 1943, RG 208, Box 3, Washington National Records Center.

reinforced almost immediately when the *Mary Ann* arrives at the already beleaguered island. Quincannon tells the commander of the marines' air force that a lot of the destruction at Hickam Field resulted from "fifth column work," to which the Leatherneck answers, "I've studied all the wars of history, gentlemen, and I've never come across any dirty treachery like that." Wishing them well as the *Mary Ann* prepares to leave after a hasty refueling, the marine tells the crew, "Go out and blast the Japs! Teach 'em that treachery can't win no matter how much of a head start it has."

Complementing the image of the Leathernecks created in *Wake Island, Air Force* shows the vastly outnumbered marine defenders bravely digging in for the Japanese assault. The island's commander acknowledges that his men are "only fighting a delaying action here." Nevertheless, he declines Quincannon's offer to fly out the wounded men, asking only for "some more Japs." Once in the air, the bomber pilot acknowledges that the marines are doomed, but tells Williams that "they're gonna have some fun before anybody gets on that island."

The *Mary Ann* does take one passenger away from Wake, a mongrel pup named Tripoli that one of the marines gave Weinberg for safekeeping. The dog, trained to go into a rage at the mention of "Mr. Moto," provides what little humor *Air Force* has. Tripoli also provides the spark for showing Winocki's changing attitude. When White complains that having the dog aboard the plane violates regulations, the gunner bitterly responds, "What difference does it make, regulations? You know why this dog is here. An' you know what chances those marines got back on that island. So do they. That's why they give us this dog. . . . I'm gettin' sore. We get chased out o' the place before we can even light. We're getting kicked around all over the place by a lot o' little sneakin' Nips an' you're yappin' your head off about regulations!" When the sergeant asks if Winocki is changing his tune, he snaps, "So what if I am? I'd like to do a little chasin' myself!"

The plane's arrival in the Philippines gives the crew the opportunity to do some chasing, but not before hearing the standard account of the Japanese attacks and the response of the outnumbered Americans: "We've taken an awful licking here because we were caught on the ground. Since then, they've outnumbered us ten to one. Yet every time we've been up against them, they've lost five to our one. In other words, if we were anywhere near equal we could lick 'em. The record proves it. And from now on, our job's to keep on fighting with what we've got until we can get enough airplanes to blast 'em off the earth."

Nothing must come in the way of that. When White learns that his pilot son had been killed in the first attack while trying to get his plane off the ground, the crew chief observes, with only a slight quiver in his voice, "Didn't even get into the air! It's not much to show for twenty years, is it, sir?" He turns and immediately goes back to work preparing the *Mary Ann* for its first encounter with the Japanese fleet. According to Triffy, the scene "was the real tearjerker in the film . . . when he was handed in the kerchief the personal effects of his son." The technical adviser recalled that casting the role had been difficult and Hawks had finally decided on Carey even though he was seventy-three and obviously too old for the character. Nevertheless, Triffy said, "Harry did a hell of a fine job," noting that, despite his age, Carey refused to use a double even when he had to simulate bailing out of the *Mary Ann* and land on a mattress.

The scene takes place after the B-17 is shot up during its initial combat mission. Taking off with only three bombs when a Japanese air strike approaches, the plane nevertheless begins a search for the enemy invasion fleet. Breaking out of the clouds, the B-17 runs into a flight of Zeros instead of the naval armada. White, fighting to hold back his grief, knocks down one of the first enemy planes in what becomes a virtual turkey shoot. Along with the visual certification of the Japanese inferiority, Weinberg provides the verbal confirmation: "Did yuh see that? They break up in little pieces. . . . Fried Jap goin' down!" Hopelessly outnumbered, however, the bomber ultimately receives more than a hundred hits and one engine catches fire. Quincannon, mortally wounded, orders the crew to bail out. Disobeying the command, Winocki stays behind and, drawing on his earlier flight training, belly-lands the *Mary Ann* back at Clark Field.

The rest of the crew arrive back at the base in time to join Winocki and Rader at Quincannon's bedside before he dies. Having promised the pilot that the *Mary Ann* will fly again, White leads the men back to the field to rebuild the bomber. Unaware of the decision to destroy the crippled planes before the advancing Japanese reach the field, the crew work all night on the bomber while also trying to locate gasoline and armaments.

When confronted with the order to destroy the bomber, the crew, led by White, convince the commander to delay his instructions, promising to burn the B-17 themselves if they cannot get it into the air before the Japanese arrive. Despite the limited time remaining to complete the repairs, Williams, now in command of the *Mary Ann*, allows Chester to volunteer to fly a brief sortie as tail gunner on an observation flight. When a Japanese Zero shoots down the plane, Chester parachutes and is machine-gunned to death in mid-air. The same kind of scene had appeared in *Wake Island*, a visual image that was to become a cliché to show Japanese barbarism.

After shooting down the plane and in turn machine-gunning to death the Japanese pilot as he tries to escape his burning ship, the crew return to work, including the installation of a tail gun, which the early-model B-17 lacked. They are joined by Rader, who had temporarily become a foot soldier after once again being shot out of the sky. The former fighter pilot manages to find gasoline and, in a race against the advancing Japanese soldiers, marines pass can after can to the waiting crew.

Before the fueling can be completed, the enemy reaches the field's perimeter. With Williams trying to keep the marines from burning the *Mary Ann*, Tex attempts to start the plane's engines. At the penultimate moment, the last one catches and the crew scramble aboard. When Williams is wounded, Rader manages to get the bomber into the air as the crew hold off the Japanese soldiers in a scene reminiscent of Indians chasing a stagecoach.

With Rader continuing at the controls, the *Mary Ann* heads toward Australia. On the way, however, it comes upon a

Japanese fleet headed in the same direction. Ducking back into the clouds, the plane radios the information to all Allied air bases and ships at sea. After circling overhead—endlessly, it seems—until a huge air armada arrives like the cavalry, the *Mary Ann* leads the strike force into the battle, which Williams says will show "what Air Force can do!" What happens next, in its own way, resembles the end of Sam Peckinpaugh's *The Wild Bunch* or *Butch Cassidy and the Sundance Kid*: wave upon wave of American planes slaughter the Japanese fleet. If the miniature work lacked the sense of complete reality, especially when intercut with some combat footage, and if the destruction was too complete to be believable, the overall impact provided the audience a catharsis for the early setbacks the United States had suffered at Pearl Harbor, Wake Island, and the Philippines. In this context, the closing shot of the battle—a Japanese flag slowly sinking beneath the waves—becomes a visual prophecy for Americans of the war's future course, rather than a trite image that might provoke humor.

Not content to end here, however, Hawks follows the saga of the *Mary Ann* on to Australia. Having lost half of the already short supply of fuel during the battle, the B-17 barely makes it to the island continent, crash-landing in the surf just off the beach in a sequence that looks remarkably authentic. The scene dissolves into one in a briefing room where an officer prepares the fliers to attack Tokyo for the first time: "This is what we've been waiting for. Tonight your target is Tokyo. And you're gonna play 'em the 'Star-Spangled Banner' with two-ton bombs." Rader, who has decided to opt for bombers, leads one section and Williams the other. Lieutenant Hauser navigates for the entire squadron and McMartin directs the bombardiers. As the formation takes off into the dusk the audience again hears Roosevelt's war message: "We shall carry the attack against the enemy. We shall hit him, and hit him again, wherever and whenever we can reach him, for we intend to bring this battle to him on his own home grounds!"

The closing images notwithstanding, bombing of Japan did not begin until 1944 (except for Jimmy Doolittle's raid in April 1942). When it did, B-29 Superfortresses carried out the bombing, not B-17s. The limited combat footage that Hawks used to give realism to his climactic battle probably came from the Midway engagement of May 1942, which led many viewers to conclude that the battle recreated the battle of the Coral Sea or Midway. In fact, the miniature shooting had been completed months before the two encounters with the Japanese fleets had occurred. And while B-17s did take part in them, the *Mary Ann*-type bombers did not cover themselves with glory as portrayed in *Air Force*. At Coral Sea, three B-17s accidentally attacked part of the American fleet but did not inflict any damage. At Midway, navy carrier-based planes carried the brunt of the attack to the Japanese fleet and sank four enemy carriers.

Response to the Film

Despite its mythical-cum-historical narrative, however, *Air Force* did more than simply entertain the American people. As General Arnold had hoped, the film conveyed the potential of bombers and the expectation that the Air Force would play a major role in the victory over Japan. Moreover, Howard Hawks's single-minded pursuit of authenticity did make the career of the *Mary Ann* and her crew seem almost real. Bosley Crowther, in the *New York Times* (February 4, 1943), wrote that the director's "boundless enthusiasm and awe" for the American fliers had enabled him to make a "picture which tingles with the passion of spirits aglow. . . . Mr. Hawks has directed the action for tremendous impact. . . . Maybe the story is high-flown, maybe it overdraws a recorded fact a bit. [But I would] hate to think it couldn't happen—or didn't—because it certainly leaves you feeling awfully good."

This "feeling awfully good" about something represents the goal of all effective propaganda. In making Americans "feel proud all over again" *Air Force* stands as one of Hollywood's brightest achievements of World War II morale-building. Its propaganda value did not make the film the box-office success it enjoyed, however. That came from the quality of the film's drama, which resulted from Hawks's careful building of tensions. According to the *Brooklyn Citizen* (April 21, 1943), the director had made a "profoundly moving and thrilling" film, "top-notch screen entertainment. . . . Very definitely it's not to be missed."

Other reviews offered the same high praise for the quality of the film, saying it provided both entertainment and morale-building. *Variety* (February 3, 1943) called *Air Force* "one of the sock war pictures of this or any other war. . . . It is gripping, informative, entertaining, thrilling. It is a patriotic heart-throb in celluloid without preaching; it is inspirational without being phoney in its emotions." The bible of the entertainment industry predicted the film "will mop up."

Perhaps the *New York Daily Mirror* (February 4, 1943) best explained why *Air Force* did mop up, becoming one of the ten top-grossing films of 1943: "The action is so furious, the scope so comprehensive, the horizon so limitless, that one sees and still one cannot grasp in full the racing, roaring, ripping rush of drama, almost unadorned by emotion other than a passion to win the war." Confirming Triffy's judgment, the reviewer commended the filmmakers "because they did not yield to the obvious temptation and clutter such a screen document with the boy-girl footage too often deemed essential in projecting tales of battling men. *Air Force* doesn't need any sex. Women should see such things, they can't live them." According to the *Mirror*, Hawks was responsible for the film's success; he "surpasses all his former triumphs. . . . What is left now for future flying pictures to shoot is a problem for the industry. This one has swept it all up."

Of films made during World War II, only *Thirty Seconds over Tokyo*, the 1944 MGM re-creation of Doolittle's raid, compares with *Air Force* in its portrayal of the war in the air. The *New York Times* and the National Board of Review both selected *Air Force* as one of the ten best films of 1943. George Amy won an Oscar for best film editing. Dudley Nichols received a nomination for best original screenplay, as did James Wong Howe, Elmer Dyer, and Charles Marshall for their black and white cinematography. Over the years, *Air Force* has become a regular feature on late-night television and in war movie retrospectives, ranking with *Thirty Seconds over Tokyo* and *Twelve O'Clock High* (20th

Century-Fox, 1949) as the most popular films about World War II in the air.

Unlike the other two films, *Air Force* does not base its continuing appeal on its re-creation of a past reality or focus on a strong central character with whom the audience can empathize. Today, the historical inaccuracies and distortions in Hawks's films are readily apparent. Its obvious propaganda aims—to promote the importance of bombers, to create within the American people the desire for revenge against a treacherous enemy, and to uphold the belief in ultimate victory—no longer have relevance. Despite the high quality of the miniature work, the scenes of the *Mary Ann* landing and taking off (which were created in the studio) clash with the footage shot in Florida. And most of the special effects sequences in the climactic battle lack visual realism, although they are certainly equal to much of the highly touted miniature work in *Tora! Tora! Tora!* Finally, the members of the B-17's crew, however well portrayed, remain only broad stereotypes who serve as supporting characters to the film's star, the *Mary Ann.*

To audiences in 1943, the *Mary Ann* symbolized the good but still-outnumbered Americans who had suffered a series of traumatic defeats by the treacherous, evil Japanese. The *Mary Ann*-led victory over the Japanese fleet did undoubtedly leave audiences "feeling awfully good" and so provided a boost to the war effort. Contemporary viewers of *Air Force,* still suffering from the nation's real or perceived defeat in Vietnam, may find much the same positive feeling when they watch Americans winning in a good war against a recognizably bad enemy. Equally important to its continuing popularity, *Air Force* does not focus on the horrors of war or its moral ambiguities as have movies on the subject of the Vietnam war. Instead, despite the necessary propaganda statements, Hawks allows several generations of viewers to become immersed in action and adventure, the ingredients of the classic Hollywood escapist war movies.

1. *The* Mary Ann *on flight line preparing to depart for Hawaii on the night of December 6, 1941.*

2. *The crusty crew chief of the* Mary Ann, *Sergeant White (Harry Carey), briefs the new second radio operator, Private Chester (Ray Montgomery).*

3. *The flight of nine B-17s heads toward Hawaii.*

4. *Captain Quincannon (John Ridgely) tries to win commitment to the* Mary Ann *and her crew from Sergeant Winocki (John Garfield), whom Quincannon had once washed out of flight school.*

5. *The* Mary Ann *in flight on the way to Wake Island.*

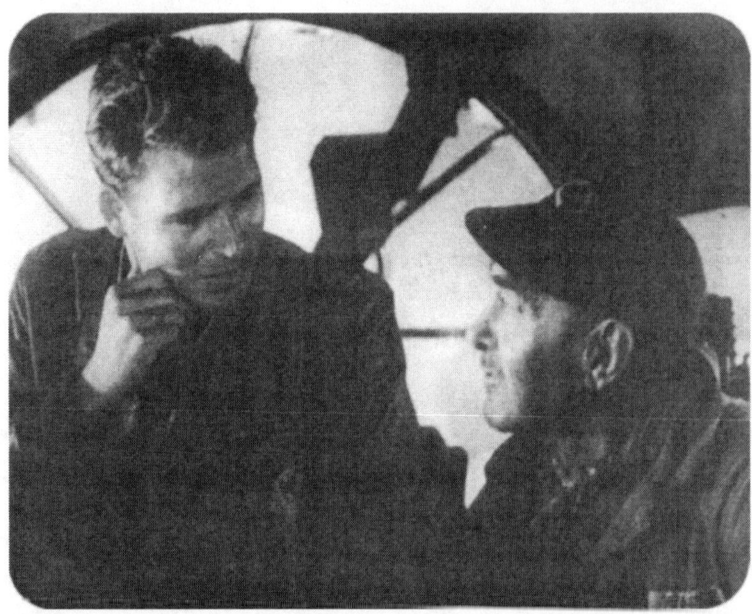

6. *Sergeant White asks the navigator, Lieutenant Hauser (Charles Drake), how the trip to Wake Island is going.*

7. Lieutenant McMartin (Arthur Kennedy), center, tells Quincannon and Lieutenant Williams (Gig Young) that his sister will recover.

8. Pursuit pilot Lieutenant Rader (James Brown) tells about the Japanese pilots he fought over Pearl Harbor: "They're pretty good when they've got the edge, ten or twelve to one. They don't like an even fight though."

9. *Winocki, Corporal Weinberg (George Tobias), and White listen to President Roosevelt's speech asking Congress to declare war.*

10. *Marines on Wake Island give Tripoli to Weinberg before the* Mary Ann *heads on to the Philippines.*

11. *The* Mary Ann *is welcomed to the Philippines by the besieged defenders.*

12. *Quincannon informs White that his son died during the first attack on the Philippines.*

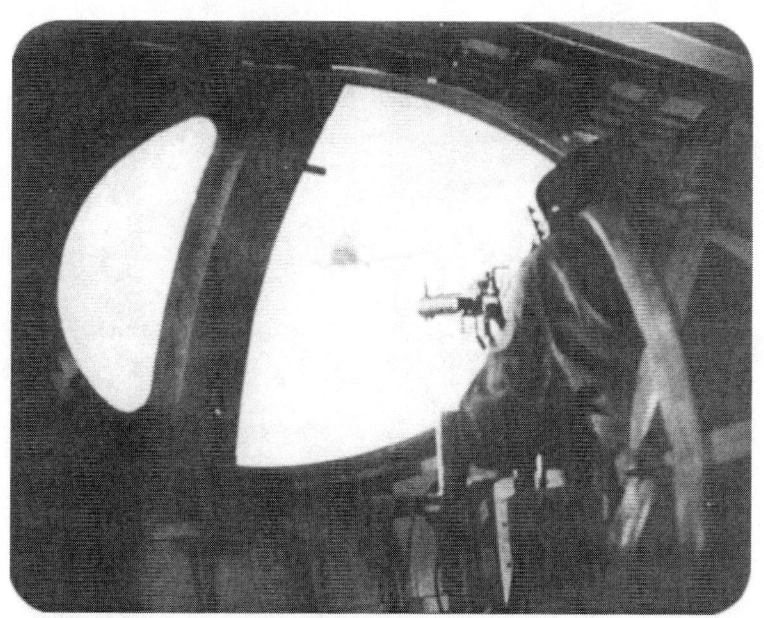

13. *Japanese planes attack the* Mary Ann.

14. *Winocki lands the crippled* Mary Ann *after the crew, except for the wounded Quincannon, have bailed out.*

15. *The crew surround the mortally wounded Quincannon.*

16. *The crew struggle to make the* Mary Ann *flyable before the Japanese overrun the field.*

17. *Rear gunner Chester is machine-gunned as he parachutes from plane.*

18. *A Japanese ship fires on the* Mary Ann *as the film's climactic battle begins.*

19. *A model of a Japanese carrier sails through a studio tank for the climactic battle, filmed before the historic battles of Coral Sea and Midway.*

20. *Japanese officers react to the sight of attacking American planes.*

21. *A Japanese ship goes up in flames.*

22. *Weinberg spots attacking Japanese fighters as Marine Sergeant Callahan (Edward Brophy) and Tripoli look on.*

23. *The* Mary Ann *sinks a carrier.*

24. *The* Mary Ann *crash-lands in the surf off the Australian coast.*

Air Force

Screenplay

by

DUDLEY NICHOLS

Air Force

FADE IN

1. CLOSE-UP TELETYPE MACHINE DAY

clattering away. Insert the printed tape feeding out of it. We read:

> Commanding officer, 48th Wing, Mather Field, Calif. SIGYF XLPTQ RLBWD—

LAP DISSOLVE:

2. CLOSE SHOT SIGN OVER DOOR

U.S. AIR CORPS
Intelligence Div.

3. INT. OFFICE MED. SHOT LIEUTENANT

at a deciphering machine as an orderly hands him the printed tape from teletype machine. The officer nods and orderly exits. Officer inserts tape in cylinder and opens an envelope marked Confidential. He looks at: Insert in big type on a sheet of paper:

> Code line for today: CHARLEY'S AUNT PREFERS FRESH OYSTERS.

4. CLOSE SHOT OFFICER

as he sets up this line on the deciphering machine and begins pressing keys. Insert message being decoded:

> Practice flight of nine B-17s will take off for Honolulu at 0200—

LAP DISSOLVE TO:

5–9. OMITTED

10–11. INT. SQUADRON ORDERLY ROOM

About a dozen young officers are seated informally

around the room listening to Roberts, who has told them of their mission. Present among others are Quincannon, Williams, McMartin, and Hauser, bunched together.

ROBERTS:
Everything clear now to the pilots? . . . Yes, Quincannon?

QUINCANNON:
Will we be flying on radio beam all the way?

ROBERTS:
Yes. To keep a double check, flight leaders will work Hickam radio control while the other airplanes work the home station. (Looks around.) How about you navigators? . . . Hauser?

HAUSER:
How soon can we get our charts and maps from Group Operations, sir?

ROBERTS:
Any time you want. You'll be given the route weather forecast as soon as it's finished. Any questions from the bombardiers? . . . Yes, McMartin?

McMARTIN:
Are we taking bombsights along?

ROBERTS (nods):
You're ferrying them fully equipped. Except for ammunition, of course. The maintenance crews are working on the ships now, so you pilots can check with them to be sure everything's in shape. I guess that's all for now. (As they get up.) Oh yes—the crews haven't been told yet what the destination is, so keep it quiet.

QUINCANNON:
Can we phone our wives?

ROBERTS:

To be sure. (With a faint smile.) Evidently your copilot doesn't take you into his confidence. He obtained permission this morning to send a radiogram to Lieutenant McMartin's sister in Honolulu. (Grins as McMartin gives Williams a look.) I thought that might interest you, McMartin. (McMartin grins at the sheepish Williams. Roberts checks over his notes to see if he's missed anything.) Well, that seems to be all for the moment. Check your airplanes thoroughly and be on the hangar line by midnight.

The officers get to their feet and begin moving out in groups of two and three. Several of them go over to Roberts to ask further questions. Camera moves in on our four as they move toward door, other officers passing them in background. McMartin turns to Williams.

McMARTIN:

Say, what about that radiogram? Why didn't you tell me? I'd have put in a few words for Susan myself.

WILLIAMS:

At two bits per word—yeah. You go send your own radios.

12. HANGAR LINE FULL SHOT FIVE IMMENSE FLYING FORTRESSES

on the line while four more are being pulled out of the hangars. Ground crews working on them. Here and there in the distance an engine is started, then stopped. In foreground a ship is pulled out on the tarmac by a small tractor. As she is pulled into place the tractor is unhooked.

13. NEAR SHOT FLYING FORTRESS

On the fuselage forward of the door we see the name Mary Ann lettered. Ground crew men swarm over the big ship, getting her ready. Williams and McMartin enter and climb into the ship for an inspection. A ladder is wheeled in on one of the engines nearest camera, and one of the crew (Weinberg) mounts it as a youngster enters with his duffle bag.

14. NEAR SHOT AT LADDER
as the kid enters and calls to Weinberg.

KID:
Corporal. Where will I find the captain?

WEINBERG (looks down):
Ain't here yet. You the new gunner?

KID:
Second radio.

WEINBERG (seeing how young he is):
Yeah? (Stoops and gives a greasy hand.) Duh name's Weinberg. Second engineer. You're a lucky kid. Dis old *Mary Ann*'s duh best ship in duh outfit. (Points off.) See dat big guy over dere in duh hangar? Dat's duh crew chief, Sergeant White. You better report to him.

KID:
Thanks, Corporal.

15. INT. HANGAR MED. SHOT SERGEANT WHITE
adding a penciled notation on Form 41, the portable file which records all work done on *Mary Ann*. The form is hung on the wall. Quincannon comes swinging along and enters.

QUINCANNON:
Everything okay, Sergeant? (Looks at form as White finishes notation.)

WHITE:
Yes, sir. I put a new magneto on number three en-

gine. (Looks at captain.) They told me to get 'er ready for a long trip.

QUINCANNON (inspecting sheet absently):
Yeah.

WHITE:
They didn't say where to, though.

QUINCANNON:
They didn't?

WHITE:
No, sir.

QUINCANNON:
Can you keep a secret?

WHITE:
Yes, sir.

QUINCANNON:
Good.

White looks disappointed as the kid enters and salutes.

KID:
Sergeant White? (White nods.) Private Chester reporting, sir. Second radio.

WHITE (sizing him up with a kindly eye):
Mmmm. You can stow your gear in the ship. This is Captain Quincannon.

KID (salutes him again unnecessarily):
I'm glad to be assigned to your airplane, sir. I've been hoping to get on a flying fortress ever since I got out of radio school.

QUINCANNON:
How long's that been, Chester?

KID:
Three months, sir. (Quickly.) But I've had experience. I've been in the light bombers.

QUINCANNON (nods as if that were great stuff):
Have you met our first radio?

KID:
No, sir.

QUINCANNON (to White):
Turn him over to Corporal Peterson. (To Kid.) You can look over the radio set with Peterson and get the hang of things. (Exits toward plane.)

KID:
What time do we take off, Sergeant?

WHITE:
Two A.M.

KID:
Must be a big flight. Nine fortresses.

WHITE:
So they say.

KID:
Do you know—I mean, can you tell me where we're going?

WHITE:
Can you keep a secret?

KID:
Yes, *sir*.

WHITE (smiles):
Good.

LAP DISSOLVE:

16. OMITTED

17. EXT. SHIP NEAR DOOR
as White comes in followed by Chester. A stocky sergeant carrying a suitcase enters and confronts him.

WINOCKI:
Crew chief?

WHITE (nods):
You our new gunner?

WINOCKI:
Yeah. Sergeant Winocki. Joe Winocki.

WHITE (offers a friendly hand):
I been expecting you, Sergeant. Put your stuff inside. You're lucky—our regular gunner's on furlough.

WINOCKI:
I wouldn't say I'm lucky.

White looks at him curiously but Winocki makes no explanation as he tosses his suitcase in the doorway and climbs in after it.

DISSOLVE TO:

18. HANGAR LINE NIGHT

FULL SHOT OF THE NINE FORTRESSES ON THE LINE

Many field lights, the tower beacon revolving, all the bright illumination of peacetime. Here and there engines are being warmed up. Ground crews are busy around the ships putting on final touches.

19–20. OMITTED

21. WIDE ANGLE ON MARY ANN

outlined brightly in floodlights. Mechanics wheel away the last of the ground gear. Peterson and Weinberg are climbing in as the four officers enter from direction of hangar. McMartin, Hauser, and Williams are climbing in as Sergeant White comes around the ship to Quincannon, who is looking around for someone.

22. MED. SHOT QUINCANNON

as White enters to him.

QUINCANNON:

Seen anything of my wife, chief?

WHITE:

Not yet, sir.

QUINCANNON (glances at watch):

That's funny. She said she'd be here by midnight. (Pulls his mind to business.) How about coffee and sandwiches?

WHITE:

Got 'em, sir.

QUINCANNON:

I wish we could get hold of an extra supply of oxygen.

WHITE:

Already in the ship, sir. Six bottles.

QUINCANNON (looks at him):

How'd you do *that?*

White just grins at him. Winocki comes along behind them to get into doorway.

WHITE:

Oh, Winocki! (Winocki turns and comes to them.) This is our new gunner, Captain. (To Winocki.) Captain Quincannon.

QUINCANNON (returns the grudging salute and looks at him closely):

Don't I know you, Sergeant?

WINOCKI:

I think you do, sir.

QUINCANNON (trying to remember):

Weren't you at Randolph Field when I was instructing there?

WINOCKI:

I think you remember. Anything else, sir?

QUINCANNON (as it all comes back):

Not now. No.

Winocki abruptly turns away and climbs into ship. White looks after him, annoyed by his manner, and then looks at Quincannon inquiringly but Quincannon isn't telling.

QUINCANNON:

Everyone on board?

WHITE:

All except the new kid. He's over there with his mother.

Both look off at:

22A. MED. LONG SHOT

The kid and his mother under a light in front of a hangar.

22B. CLOSE TWO-SHOT WHITE AND QUINCANNON

watching them.

QUINCANNON:

Nice kid, Sergeant.

WHITE:

We're gettin' 'em just off the bottle nowadays.

QUINCANNON (his eyes grin):

We were all pretty young when we started out, grandpa. How old is that kid of *yours* you're always talking about?

WHITE (has to grin):

About that age—twenty-one. (With pride.) Think of it—me saluting my own kid.

QUINCANNON:

You'd bat his ears down if he didn't take it. Where's he stationed now?

WHITE:

Clark Field, Manila. (Very proud.) He's a full-fledged pilot, sir.

QUINCANNON (grins at him):

If he gets another bar on his shoulders you'll need a bigger hat, Robbie. (Glances at watch.) Well, think I'll take one last look for Mary. Back in a minute. (Walks off.)

23. IN FRONT OF HANGAR MED. SHOT
PRIVATE CHESTER AND HIS MOTHER
a pleasant vigorous woman of forty-odd. She has given the kid a packet of sandwiches.

MRS. CHESTER:

I put in a piece of that cake you like.

KID:

Thanks, Mom. (Looks off at plane.) I better be going now.

MRS. CHESTER:

You haven't told me yet where you're going, Henry.

KID (feeling pretty big):

We're not supposed to tell.

MRS. CHESTER (smiles at him, trying to find out as she would from the small boy he used to be):

Pshaw. I suppose next week I'll be getting a letter from San Diego.

KID (shakes head importantly):

Maybe it's Florida. (His imagination on wings.) Or even the Panama *Canal*.

MRS. CHESTER (wide-eyed):
Well, *which?*

KID:
Can you keep a secret, Mom?

MRS. CHESTER:
Of course I can!

KID:
Good. (Grins as she looks at him with vexation.) Here comes our captain. Would you like to meet him?

He is off even before she answers.

24. NEAR HANGAR
as Quincannon walks into camera, looking around for his wife. The kid intercepts him, entering from the side, but not so boldly as he set off from his mother.

KID:
Excuse me, sir. (As Quincannon stops and turns.) My mother would like to meet you, Captain. Would you mind if— (Hesitates.)

QUINCANNON:
Certainly, Chester. (Turns off with the kid.)

25. MED. SHOT MRS. CHESTER
as Quincannon enters pleasantly with the kid and salutes and takes the hand she offers.

QUINCANNON:
How do you do, Mrs. Chester. Mighty nice of you to turn out this time of night and see us off. I wish my wife were as punctual as you are.

MRS. CHESTER (puts her hand on the kid's arm):
I hope you'll look after this boy of mine.

KID (dying of embarrassment):
Gee—*Mother*.

QUINCANNON (saving him):
He'll be looking after me, too, Mrs. Chester. We're all one team—we look after each other. That's why we always come through. (Glances at his watch, then at the kid.) We won't need you for two minutes more. Good night, Mrs. Chester. Don't worry about our radio man. He'll be back in a couple of weeks with a good tan.

MRS. CHESTER (gratefully):
Thank you, Captain. Goodbye.

As he exits Mrs. Chester looks at her son and her hand tightens on his arm as if she wanted to keep him from going. She chokes up a little.

MRS. CHESTER:
Oh, my dear boy. You're all I've got.

KID (awkwardly):
I'll write to you, Mom—so you'll know where I am.

MRS. CHESTER (chokes a little):
Be a good boy, Henry.

KID:
I will, Mom. (Kisses her swiftly and awkwardly.) G'bye, Mom.

And he hurries out toward ship, the package under his arm. She stands watching after him with emotion.

26. NEAR AIRPLANE MED. SHOT SERGEANT WHITE
standing by fuselage where the name Mary Ann is painted, as Quincannon enters, glancing at his watch.

WHITE:
No luck, sir?

QUINCANNON (shakes head):
Looks like I've been ditched, Robbie. (As both look off hopefully the kid comes hurrying in. White motions him into the ship.)

WHITE:
Get aboard, Chester. (Looks at Quincannon who is taking a last look off.)

QUINCANNON:
Well, let's go.

White climbs in and Quincannon is following when a woman's voice is heard calling:

MARY'S VOICE:
Irish! Wait a minute, *Irish!*

Quincannon turns and jumps down to ground quickly as Mary Quincannon comes running in breathlessly with their year-and-a-half-old son scooped in her arms.

QUINCANNON:
Well, it's about time, Mrs. Quincannon. What happened? Have another date?

MARY (breathlessly):
Flat tire. Ever try to get a taxi this time of night? I was scared stiff I wouldn't make it.

QUINCANNON (takes the baby proudly):
Hiya, fella. (The baby waves a toy clutched in its hands.)

MARY:
Look—he wants to give you his lucky pilot.

QUINCANNON:
Okay, laddybucks—I'll take it along for a mascot. (As he takes it the baby makes weird noises and they laugh.)

MARY:
Hear that? He's saying happy landings.

QUINCANNON (grins):
You two have a language all your own. I don't get the hang of it.

MARY:
Oh, darling, couldn't we stow away?

QUINCANNON:
Want to get me court-martialed?

MARY (makes a face):
I'm jealous of *Mary Ann.*

QUINCANNON (teasingly):
She's big and blonde and beautiful, all right.

MARY:
I believe you love her more than you do me.

QUINCANNON:
Only in the air, honey. On the ground I belong to you and this cuss.

WHITE (calls from door out of scene):
One minute to go, sir!

QUINCANNON (off):
Okay, Sergeant. (To Mary.) I'll be back in a couple of weeks and we'll take time off for that honeymoon.

MARY:
Blarney! I can remember every honeymoon we didn't take—even the first one.

QUINCANNON (slips his free arm around her):
You oughta be glad the way things are—you never have time to get bored with me.

MARY:
I'll *never* get bored with you, Irish. It's been fun—every minute of it. Oh, such fun. I'm a lucky girl.

QUINCANNON (gruffly):
I'm a lucky guy.

They are beyond words as they look at each other. Sergeant White enters reluctantly.

WHITE:
Two o'clock, sir.

MARY (her eyes too bright and her voice suddenly husky):
Sergeant— (White looks at her and she forces a smile.) He's six feet one but he often forgets to put on his rubbers when he goes out in the rain. Look after him, will you?

WHITE:
Sure I will.

MARY (huskily):
And bring him back to me.

WHITE:
Sure, Mrs. Quincannon. Don't you worry.

QUINCANNON (pulls Mary around to him):
Hey, who's looking after who? I'm running this outfit. (Mary doesn't answer, just looks at him as White turns out of scene. They look at each other deeply, seriously, saying things no words can say. Silently he hands her the baby and she takes it but keeps looking at him.) So long, kid.

MARY (whispers):
So long, Irish. Happy landings.

He kisses her and abruptly she turns away toward the hangar, afraid he will see her crying, and Quincannon follows White to the door of the ship.

27–29. INCLUDED IN FOREGOING

30. INT. MARY ANN TRUCK SHOT ALONG CROSS SECTION so we get an idea of the layout of the airplane's interior. First camera is within, shooting at door. Sergeant White, already in, gives Quincannon a hand. Winocki and the kid are in this door section, and they make room as Quincannon swings in. Winocki watches Quincannon out of the corner of his eye as the captain starts forward and White shuts the door and bolts it behind him. Camera trucks along on Quincannon as he steps over transom into radio compartment, bringing into view Peterson already at his radio desk and Weinberg in the seat opposite. Truck on Quincannon as he steps over transom into bomb bay where two spare fuel tanks replace the bomb load. We can just see his head and his feet, moving along the narrow catwalk. Then he steps over transom and is in full view in the control compartment or cockpit. Williams is already in the copilot's seat. The hatch behind pilots' seat is open and McMartin's head appears. Quincannon grins at McMartin.

QUINCANNON:

Get down in that meat can, Tommy. Be useful. Keep the navigator awake.

McMARTIN:

Okay, sir—you flathead.

His head disappears into bombardier's compartment, and Quincannon steps over the hatch and slides into his seat. The first thing he does is to hang up the little toy by the piece of string which is attached to it. Williams is sliding on his headphones, watching as Sergeant White comes into compartment and takes his place behind the pilot.

WILLIAMS:

What's *that* for?

QUINCANNON (grins):

That's from Michael Aloysius Quincannon, Junior.

(To White as he pulls on his headphones.) Hit the wobble pump, Sergeant.

WHITE:

She's pretty warm, sir. Won't need much priming. Couple of shots.

WILLIAMS:

Switch on your radio. Flight commander's calling.

Quincannon throws the switch at his side and immediately we hear Roberts's voice.

RADIO:

Major Roberts to flight. Start engines!

Quincannon starts the engines and we hear them catch and then roar as they rev up. White leans over, watching dials and listening closely. Those engines are his babies and he shows it. Above the roar we hear the radio again.

RADIO:

Zero one one zero four to control tower—

31–32. INT. CONTROL TOWER

The control officer stands watching out a window through which we can see the nine fortresses pulsing on the line, their big props gleaming in the floodlights. Roberts's voice continues over cut:

RADIO:

Zero one one zero four to control tower—

CONTROL OFFICER (into hand mike):

Tower to zero one one zero four. Go ahead.

ROBERTS'S VOICE:

Takeoff instructions for flight of nine airplanes.

CONTROL OFFICER:

Okay to taxi up to north end of ramp. Use runway two eight. Wind—dog, victor. Go ahead.

33. INT. COCKPIT OF MARY ANN

Quincannon is revving up the engines, touching this and that control as Roberts's voice comes over radio.

RADIO:

Zero one one zero four to flight. All planes follow me. Runway twenty-eight. Wind—dog, victor. Clear at fifteen-second intervals.

As Quincannon pushes up the throttles and the four great engines roar, *Mary Ann* begins to move out, and through the windows we see other ships rolling out with muffled thunder.

34. INT. CONTROL TOWER

Through the window past the control officer we see the flight rolling out.

CONTROL OFFICER:

Tower to zero one one zero four. Clear when ready.

ROBERTS'S VOICE:

Zero one one zero four—roger.

35. RUNWAY QUICK EXCITING SHOTS

of a fortress taking off, then another, then still another.

36. INT. COCKPIT OF MARY ANN

Now the pilots are "pouring on coal," and the big ship is thundering forward and shaking and shivering as she gathers speed. Through windows we see field lights whip past. As the roar reaches a tremendous pitch and lights are mere streaks, suddenly she lifts and we feel the sudden smoothness as she climbs. The tower beacon swings past and for an instant brightly lights the three faces.

QUINCANNON:

Wheels up!

Williams pulls a switch that retracts landing gear.

37. SHOT UNDER PLANE SHOWING THE HUGE WHEELS
retracting into body of ship. The beacon wipes past again with a flash of bright light.

38. INT. COCKPIT
Quincannon, watching a thousand things at once, is pulling back throttles. Williams reducing propellor rpm to climb position. White doing what he can to help. Through Plexiglas windows we see other ships. *Mary Ann* moves into position behind the three ships that look off ahead. A few seconds later two wingmen slide in behind *Mary Ann.*

39. GROUND CLOSE TWO-SHOT MARY QUINCANNON AND MRS. CHESTER
watching up at:

40. SKY SHOT THE NINE FORTRESSES
moving shot into formation, their lights still on, sparkling beautifully against the moonlit sky.

41. CLOSE SHOT MARY ANN
flying, the camera catching her name. Her great motors pulsing.

42. INT. COCKPIT CLOSE ON PILOTS
White standing just behind them and helping them synchronize the engines. Quincannon finally gets them smoothed out and we notice the difference in their sound. Quincannon looks around at White, complimenting him in an offhand way.

QUINCANNON:

They sound pretty sweet, Sergeant.

WHITE:

Thank you, sir. Anything more?

Quincannon shakes his head and White turns aft to look through the ship. Now we hear Roberts's voice over radio.

RADIO:

Climbing at thirty inches and two thousand. Remember we have a slight head wind. Watch your fuel flow.

As White exits McMartin crawls up through the hatch and stands behind the pilots. He touches Williams on the shoulder.

McMARTIN:

Did you get any reply from Susan?

QUINCANNON (dryly):

Watch out, Tommy—the boy is burning.

McMARTIN:

What's the matter?

WILLIAMS (turns and looks him in the eye):

Did you know Tex Rader's stationed at Hickam Field?

McMARTIN (nods):

Don't let that bother you. I wrote Sue to watch out for him—he's a load of hot air.

WILLIAMS (bitterly):

He's a pain in the pants.

McMARTIN (stares at him as Irish grins):

Don't tell me she turned you down for that Texas peashooter!

WILLIAMS:

No, but I don't trust him. He knows I'm as good as engaged to your sister—and look what I get. (Fishes out a crumpled radiogram.)

McMARTIN:

From *Susan?*

WILLIAMS (bitterly):

Read it.

McMartin does so as Quincannon grins.

43. INSERT RADIOGRAM

> Dear Williams: Have dated Miss McMartin for duration of her visit. How can a slow bomber pilot expect to beat the time of a pursuit pilot? Tex.

44. CLOSE THREE-SHOT

McMartin reacts almost as indignantly as Williams, who watches him as he takes back the radiogram. Quincannon grins as he watches them out of the corner of his eye.

QUINCANNON:

I kind of miss Tex Rader—we used to have a lot of fun at March Field.

WILLIAMS:

Fun, huh? I thought you were pretty sore that time he tried to make a grandstand landing and flew smack into us.

QUINCANNON:

That was an accident.

McMARTIN:

Yeah, and I suppose it was an accident when he swiped my girl and then shipped me a crate of lemons COD.

WILLIAMS:

Another accident—sending my name *and* photograph to all those matrimonial agencies! (Wrathfully.) I *still* get letters from middle-aged widows who'd like to take a flier!

QUINCANNON:

Have you forgotten what you did to *him?* (Grins as he looks down.) Take a last look, boys—San Francisco.

WILLIAMS (growls):
I got my eye on Honolulu![1]

45. INT. RADIO SECTION

Sergeant White is fixing something while Peterson and Weinberg are peering down through window at San Francisco. Peterson has his headphones on and is munching an apple from a large paper sack on his desk.

PETERSON:
Look—there's the Golden Gate. Christmas crackers, she's a big town, San Francisco.

WEINBERG:
Strictly a one-whistle stop. Dey's only one city in duh U.S.A. and dat's New York.

WHITE (straightens up goodnaturedly):
You're just another hometown hick, Weinberg. What's wrong with California?

WEINBERG (jeers):
California? Duh sun shines and nothin' ever happens and one day you wake up and you're sixty, dat's what.

WHITE (working at something else):
No different from New York. My sister's been trying to get out of Brooklyn for the last forty years.

WEINBERG:
Brooklyn! Dat ain't New York, Chief. Say, when you cross Brooklyn Bridge you're out of dis world. Duh only sound you can hear is duh hardening of arteries. When I was drivin' a hack I had a pal who crossed dat bridge back in 1929 and ain't been heard from since.

PETERSON (bites into apple):
What's the matter with Minneapolis?

WEINBERG:

Minneapolis? Dey's grass growin' in duh streets. Besides, dat ain't your hometown, Peterson. Duh hayseed's still stickin' outa your hair.

PETERSON (grins):

I can still milk a cow and I bet you can't.

WEINBERG:

I'll get mine out of a bottle. Dat's as close as I wanta come to a cow.

WHITE:

You're pretty handy with the bull.

Sergeant White takes an amused look at Weinberg and, taking some gear he has gathered up, steps over transom into door section aft. Camera follows to take in Winocki and the kid, who are watching out of a window. The kid is thrilled, Winocki in a bad humor. White working near them.

WINOCKI:

How far you think you're gonna get as an enlisted man?

KID (eagerly):

A lot of enlisted men get commissions. Look at the training we get—and the *experience.*

WINOCKI (shakes head):

If you can't get through Randolph you don't rate *anything*.

KID:

What about this flight?

WINOCKI:

What about it?

KID:

Why, there's a million fellows down there would give anything to be in our shoes right now.

WINOCKI (as White raises his head, listening):
Me, I'm through with the Army. My enlistment's up in another three weeks.

WHITE:
You stick to what you believe in, kid.

WINOCKI:
What are you gonna be some day—a brigadier?

WHITE:
No, but my boy is. Him and me, we kinda like the Air Corps. (Gruffly to the kid.) You stick to your guns, son. (Goes on aft into tail.)

LAP TO:

46. SHOT FROM CAMERA PLANE
on the nine airplanes flying in formation in the moonlight, leveled off at about eight thousand feet above the shining Pacific.

47. NEAR SHOT FROM CAMERA PLANE
on *Mary Ann* pulsing along.

48. INT. COCKPIT
Quincannon and Williams flying the ship as Winocki enters and comes behind them. Leans over to Quincannon with an I-won't-give-an-inch expression.

WINOCKI:
Crew chief said you wanted to see me.

Quincannon nods, makes a sign to Williams, who takes over. Quincannon turns around and they look at each other.

QUINCANNON:
I just want to get things straight with you, Winocki.

WINOCKI:
I think I'm straight. I don't know about you.

QUINCANNON (keeps his temper):
You were the cadet who cut the tail off Lieutenant Driscoll's airplane. That was an accident.

WINOCKI:
For which you washed me out of the school. I'd have been flying one of these if it hadn't been for that.

QUINCANNON (patiently):
I didn't wash you out. The board washed you out.

WINOCKI:
On your recommendation.

QUINCANNON (looks him straight in the eye):
You lacked flying ability. You should have been eliminated sooner. But I want you to know that no one held you responsible for Driscoll's death.

WINOCKI:
Except you, sir.

QUINCANNON:
Not me, either. Get that out of your head. (With sincerity.) We have two other men in this ship who washed out as pilots. McMartin became a bombardier, Hauser went in for navigation—and they're both crackerjacks. I'm glad you had the spunk to stick with it, too, and go in for gunnery.

WINOCKI (not having any):
Anything else, sir?

QUINCANNON:
Yes. Get this into your head—we all belong to this airplane. We're a single *team*. Each one of us has got to rely on every other man doing the right thing at the right time. Teamwork is all that counts. You used to play football, you ought to know. I happen to be running the team, that's all.

WINOCKI:

I happen to be a *tail* gunner, Captain. You haven't got a tail gun in this B-17. I trained in a better ship.

QUINCANNON (grimly):

This is the best airplane in the whole cockeyed world, Winocki. That's all.

Winocki turns away and goes aft stiffly and Quincannon looks at Williams who is pretty mad himself. Williams shakes his head. Quincannon grimly takes back the controls, thinking how to deal with this problem. Switches over to interphone.

QUINCANNON:

Pilot to radio operator.

49. INT. RADIO SECTION

Peterson at desk lays down the apple he is munching as he puts mikes to his throat. Weinberg, White, and the kid are sitting around.

PETERSON:

Radio operator to pilot. Go ahead.

QUINCANNON:

I'll stay on the command set, Peterson. You can cut in on broadcast frequencies if you want to give the crew a little farewell entertainment.

PETERSON:

Yes, sir. Thanks.

He turns some switches and dials and through a medley of voices we suddenly hear very clearly a news broadcaster.

RADIO:

San Francisco—Mr. Litvinov, the new Russian ambassador to the United States, arrived here yesterday on the *China Clipper* and departed immediately for the nation's capital to confer with the president.

> Washington, D.C.— Tension in the Pacific and the Far East has relaxed as a result of the peaceful mission of Japan's special envoy, Mr. Saburo Kurusu. Mr. Kurusu and Admiral Nomura have assured the press that Japan's intentions are wholly peaceful. They will meet again tomorrow morning with Secretary of State Hull.

Peterson twists dial and a band program comes in. Nobody pays much attention to the radio.

50. INT. MEAT CAN
McMartin stretches out for a sleep as Hauser takes a star shot with his octant. Then Hauser sits down at his desk, picks up a pencil, and begins to write on navigator's log. (Music from radio.)

51. INSERT HIS PENCIL
writing in a firm hand: "Position at 0224, December 7th—"

52. CLOSE SHOT HAUSER
as he goes on writing.

53. FLIGHT OF NINE PLANES
as seen from camera plane. Pan shot as they recede high over the moonlit sea toward Hawaii.

FADE OUT

FADE IN

54. THE NINE PLANES IN FORMATION
from camera plane. A vast lonely effect, the sun rising over the sea, astern of them.

55. NEAR SHOT MARY ANN
flying smooth in formation.

56. INSERT CHART OF THE PACIFIC
A pencil draws a line to the island of Oahu, tiny in the vast expanse of ocean.

57. CLOSE SHOT HAUSER
at his desk in the meat can as he finishes laying out the course and puts down his pencil.

58. OMITTED

59. INT. RADIO SECTION
Peterson at radio desk. Weinberg looking out at the ocean. Winocki in the other chair keeping his own counsel, as White comes in from the catwalk and pours coffee for himself.

WEINBERG:
How we doin', Sergeant?

WHITE:
Won't be long before you'll see Diamond Head stickin' outa that ocean.

WEINBERG:
Suits Weinberg. (Stares out at vast sea.) I used to dream about gettin' outa duh traffic jams and goin' someplace where a guy would have some elbowroom—but dis is overdoin' it. Two t'ousand miles and not a fish in sight.

PETERSON:
I kind of like it. Like bein' on the prairie when I was a kid.

WEINBERG (stares out):
Funny t'ing, I always t'ought dey was nothin' west of Manhattan except Joisey.

The kid enters along catwalk.

KID:
Say, I was just talking to the navigator. You know who his father was?

WHITE:
Sure—Monk Hauser.

WEINBERG:
Who's *dat?*

WINOCKI:
How old were *you* in the last war?

WEINBERG:
Older'n you, buddy—I was across—in duh old sixty-ninth.

WINOCKI:
Don't you ever read the papers? Monk Hauser was in Rickenbacker's squadron.

WEINBERG:
Well, whaddye know? Dat's Hauser's old man?

WHITE (nods):
Great fighter—I knew him. He had high score till they shot him down.

WEINBERG:
Why ain't dis kid of his a *pilot?*

WHITE:
He tried too hard.

WEINBERG:
Huh?

WHITE:
Ever think of what it means to be a hero's son? You can't grow up easy and natural, like our pilots did. You know you got to be good the first time you climb in an airplane—and that breaks up your nerves. (Shakes head.) Maybe we're lucky. My old man was a baseball umpire and I got used to seeing the bleachers throw pop bottles at 'im.

WEINBERG:
You got somet'ing dere, chief. My old man slugged Battlin' Siki once in a barroom—but he wasn't no hero. Guess I'm lucky he didn't slug Dempsey.

WHITE:
I guess you are—you and him both.

PETERSON:
Sergeant! (They all look around.) Something wrong with the radio. She went dead.

WHITE:
Don't tell *me*. Report it to the captain.

PETERSON:
Radio operator to pilot.

60. INT. COCKPIT
Quincannon and Williams relaxed as Quincannon switches over.

QUINCANNON:
Go ahead, Peterson.

PETERSON'S VOICE:
Hickam radio control just went off the air, sir—right in the middle of a weather report.

QUINCANNON:
Anything wrong with your set?

PETERSON:
No, sir. Doesn't seem to be.

QUINCANNON:
Hold on, I'll try liaison. (Switches to radio.) Number four to Major Roberts. Number four to Major Roberts.

RADIO:
Roberts to number four. Stand by a minute. No reception here from Hickam Field. All airplanes stand by. (Begins call.) Zero one one zero four to Hickam radio control. Zero one one zero four to Hickam radio control. (Over his voice comes hissing static and then a sharp commanding voice.) *Hickam*

radio control to zero one one zero four! Silence your radio! We are being attacked by hostile planes!

Startled reactions on faces of pilots.

61. INT. MEAT CAN

McMartin has scrambled to his feet, pressing his headphones to his ears, as he and Hauser look at each other incredulously. Roberts's voice cuts in, sharp and startled.

RADIO:

Zero one one zero four to Hickam radio control! Flight of nine airplanes coming in for landing! Any instructions?

62. INT. RADIO SECTION

White, Weinberg, and the kid are leaning over Peterson, pressing phones to their ears as the sharp commanding voice comes in again over static. Winocki alone seems unconcerned.

RADIO (in rising pitch):

Cut off your radio! Do not land here. Keep away from— (Interrupted by a shattering explosion.)

White, Weinberg, and Peterson look at each other with bewildered faces.

63. INT. COCKPIT CLOSE ON QUINCANNON AND WILLIAMS

no less stunned as Roberts's voice cuts in swiftly:

RADIO:

Roberts to flight. Spread out and make for emergency fields. Number one, take north end. Number nine, south—others in between! Silence radios! You're on your own now!

QUINCANNON:

Roger!

64. INT. MEAT CAN

McMartin and Hauser look at each other with bewilderment. Tommy switches to interphone.

MCMARTIN:

Bombardier to pilot. Say, what kind of maneuver is this? What's going on?

QUINCANNON'S VOICE:

Shut up, Tommy! *Listen!*

65. INT. RADIO SECTION

White, Weinberg, and the kid are in frozen postures around Peterson, who is adjusting dials, searching the frequencies. Winocki leans back in his chair, watching them with ironic amusement. Suddenly out of the squealing sounds and static noises the radio comes to hysterical life—excited voices, bursts of machine guns, explosions, roaring engines—all far away and indistinct.

RADIO (different voices crowded on each other):

Give 'er the needle, Bob—they're coming in again! Where'd that big formation go? There they are—about eight thousand over Diamond Head! Get off the ground, Jim—they're comin' in again! *Get off!* Watch out! There's another formation—over Pearl Harbor! Hi—look out—there's one on your tail! I can't see the— (Machine gun burst.) Can you see him now? I smacked 'im! (Roar of engine and explosion.) Stay with 'em, Bob—I'm going back for more confetti! (Machine gun burst.) *I got one!* (Another burst.) Hey, somebody get 'em off my tail! Look out, Tex—back of you! *Dive!* (Motor roars.) I'm takin' this baby with me! (Machine gun burst.)

WINOCKI:

Hey, Peterson—who're you tuned in on? Orson Welles?

WHITE:

Shut up! (Winocki only grins as White jumps forward.)

RADIO (continuing):

I got 'im, Bob! Look at 'im go! (Machine guns.) Jump, Tex! *Bail out! You're on fire!*

66. INT. COCKPIT

Quincannon and Williams listening tautly as White comes plunging through and leans close to them. The radio voices and sounds continue, unintelligible at times because of static and explosions.

WHITE:

Sounds like some bush league is tryin' to steal first base, don't it?

QUINCANNON (the radio chatters):

What's that—Chinese? (The chattering voices swell up for a moment in splashes of Japanese broken by gun bursts.)

WILLIAMS:

Japs!

QUINCANNON (to White):

Man all stations! Get the crew to their guns!

WHITE:

We've got no ammunition!

QUINCANNON:

No one knows that but us. Stick to your guns as if they were loaded— (Cuts on interphone as White exits swiftly.) Pilot to crew— Keep your eyes peeled, fellows.

67. INT. RADIO SECTION PETERSON

glued to the radio, which continues its jabbering sounds and explosions. Winocki, Weinberg, and the kid around him. White hurries in during the following:

QUINCANNON'S VOICE:

If we run into any Japs let 'em see you in the turrets. Like you're waiting for 'em. Sergeant White will man the top turret—Chester, bottom turret—Winocki, take over one of the waist guns—Weinberg, the other. Stand by on the radio, Peterson, but don't use the transmitter.

WHITE (motions Winocki and Weinberg aft):

Get on those guns.

QUINCANNON'S VOICE:

Remember we've got plenty of good fighting airplanes at Hickam Field, fellows. Just figure this is another maneuver. We'll fly her down okay.

WINOCKI:

Who does that guy think he is—Patrick Henry?

WHITE (angrily):

Take this parachute and get on that gun!

WINOCKI:

Giving us that shot of red, white, and blue whiskey! This is just a drill and he knows it!

WHITE:

You're off base, Winocki—but don't put this on if you don't want to. (Climbs into top turret as Winocki follows Weinberg aft scornfully.)

68. INT. COCKPIT CLOSE ON QUINCANNON AND WILLIAMS

QUINCANNON:

Pilot to navigator. What do you find on the chart?

69. INT. MEAT CAN HAUSER
bent over his chart.

HAUSER:

Looks like our best bet is on Maui. Turn to one hundred twenty degrees till I figure out the course.

70. INT. COCKPIT

QUINCANNON:

One hundred twenty degrees she is. (Puts the plane around.)

71. LONG SHOT OF THE NINE FORTRESSES

We see them all turning off as they spread out and break formation.

DISSOLVE SLOWLY

72. EMERGENCY FIELD ON MAUI FULL SHOT

MARY ANN NIGHT

Behind the big airplane we see thick jungle, palms and trees outlined against the moonlit sky. Men are clustered together on the ground, working at the landing gear—White, Winocki, Weinberg, Peterson, and the kid. From the surrounding darkness we hear the chirring of insects and booming of giant frogs.

73. OMITTED

74. CLOSE GROUP SHOT

on the working men. Weinberg is flat on his back under the axle, Peterson bent over him, both pulling on a wrench. Others helping, White superintending. There is no sound except for their heavy breathing and grunts and they keep glancing off uneasily—an atmosphere of apprehension. The kid who is on lookout suddenly hears something we cannot hear and calls quickly.

KID:

Sergeant! (White straightens up quickly and the kid points off nervously.) Something moving in that canebrake. (They all listen, even Weinberg sitting up.)

WEINBERG:

What is it, chief?

WHITE (under his breath):
Shut up.

The kid touches his arm and points past camera, and White nods and slides his automatic out of its holster. Now we can hear the crashing in the canebrake out of scene.

75. EDGE OF CANEBRAKE
The thrashing is loud and we can see the cane waving, and then two bedraggled figures push through into camera—Williams and Hauser.

76. CLOSE GROUP SHOT
All watching. White has his automatic half raised when he recognizes them and drops his arm. The kid looks relieved.

WEINBERG (sings out):
Why, it's duh lieutenants!

77. ANOTHER ANGLE ON GROUP
as Williams and Hauser enter and White slides his automatic back into its holster.

WHITE:
Did you find the other field, sir?

WILLIAMS (with a worried look):
Yeah, but no ammunition there either. Where's the Captain?

WHITE (indicates ship):
Still listening on the radio.

Williams strides under the wing followed by Hauser, something on his mind.

78. EXT. SHIP AT DOOR
Williams and Hauser enter and Williams turns on a flashlight and throws beam into ship.

WILLIAMS:
Irish!

QUINCANNON (appears in doorway):
Find the other field, Bill?

WILLIAMS:
Yeah. No ammunition.

QUINCANNON (swings down beside them):
How many of our flight there?

WILLIAMS:
Two. Busted up a bit but okay.

QUINCANNON:
Then we didn't lose an airplane. Roberts and five others made it to Hawaii.

WILLIAMS:
That's worth hearing. What's doing on the radio?

QUINCANNON:
Nothing since noon.

HAUSER:
Sound bad at Hickam Field?

QUINCANNON (with an intonation that makes it *very* bad):
Yeah . . . bad.

WILLIAMS (looks around to see the men are out of earshot and drops voice):
We were fired on.

QUINCANNON (looks closely):
What d'you mean?

WILLIAMS:
Just that. *Fired* on.

HAUSER:
We saw a bunch of men in a cane field and headed

for 'em to ask the way. All at once they began blazing away with rifles.

WILLIAMS (as Quincannon and McMartin stare):
Local Japs. Nice friendly fellows.

McMARTIN:
What'd you *do*, Bill?

WILLIAMS:
What d'you suppose we did? We ran like blazes!

For a moment they look at each other with anxiety. Quincannon reaches for the flashlight Williams holds.

QUINCANNON:
Gimme that flash. (Takes it and strides forward, the others following.)

79. CLOSE GROUP SHOT MEN WORKING ON LANDING GEAR
Peterson and the kid are helping with the work as Quincannon enters followed by the other three.

QUINCANNON (flows flash beam on the group):
How you coming, Sergeant?

WHITE (straightens up from where he stoops):
She'll *hold* all right but I don't know if she'll retract. (To Weinberg.) Get that cotter key in! Gimme that spanner!

Quincannon hands the kid the burning flashlight, and the kid holds it on the repaired part as Quincannon stoops down to inspect it.

QUINCANNON:
Too bad I sent her down so hard.

WHITE (grunting as he spreads cotter key):
I wonder you got in at all, sir. This field wasn't built for *Mary Ann*—

A rifle cracks and the bullet sings off a piece of metal

beside them with an ugly whine as the kid drops the burning flashlight and cries out.

QUINCANNON:

Douse that light! (White pounces on it and everything goes dark.) *Are you hurt, Chester?*

KID:

No, sir!

There is another rifle crack from the cane field nearby and the smack of the bullet into fuselage and the tinkle of something breaking. At the same moment we dimly see Winocki come tearing under the wing past them toward the field, jerking out his automatic.

QUINCANNON:

Winocki! (Grabs him.) You go crashing into that cane field and they'll chop you down! (To White.) Sergeant—clear the ship for takeoff! (Yells as rifle cracks again.) *Inside everybody!*

At that instant, with running confusion in the semidarkness, Winocki breaks away from Quincannon. But Sergeant White with wonderful agility jumps after him as if he were tagging a runner at home plate, and we see him swing as he catches Winocki on the button. Then White and Quincannon drag the inert Winocki between them under the wing. The rifle cracks again and the bullet whines off metal.

80. INT. SHIP AT DOOR

Men are piling in. Peterson, Hauser, McMartin, and Williams are already in. The latter two stand at door and swing in the others, first the kid, then Quincannon, who dashes forward out of scene. Then Weinberg and White lift the inert Winocki, and those inside drag him in as White and Weinberg follow. White is locking the door, the rifles cracking outside, as we hear the engines cough and start.

81. INT. COCKPIT

Quincannon starts the second pair of engines as Williams plunges in and slides into other seat. Yells at Quincannon as rifle cracks outside.

WILLIAMS:

You won't clear those trees in the dark!

QUINCANNON:

We got in, didn't we?

He shoves the throttles and the engines thunder, drowning even the rifle shots now. Williams stares ahead frozenly as the ship bounces and shivers as she begins to roll forward. White plunges in behind them and grips the chair-backs. Now the roar of engines is deafening and the ship jounces horribly. Palm fronds and trees begin to whip past the windows.

82. INT. RADIO SECTION

Peterson, Weinberg, the kid—all gripping on to handholds and waiting for the crash. Winocki sprawled on the floor unconscious. Weinberg with a scared face yells to Peterson as he points down at Winocki.

WEINBERG:

I wisht *I* was in dat condition!

83. INT. MEAT CAN

Hauser and McMartin hanging on and waiting for the crash. Trees whipping past. Through the nose we see what seems a forest wall ahead. The ship is going like an arrow now and rocking and pounding.

84. SHOT FROM GROUND

Ship goes thundering toward the trees as she lifts from the ground. At that moment the lights are turned on and we see trees between us and the ship. By some miracle she lifts and clears and rises through one open spot with only inches to spare.

85. INT. COCKPIT

Quincannon turns his head and grins sweatily at the hardly breathing Williams. White, hardly believing it, leans over and pats Quincannon on the back. Quincannon grins and pats the toy hanging beside him.

86. INT. RADIO SECTION

The men are rigid, hardly breathing, not daring to look out. Winocki still sprawled on the floor, dead to the world. Peterson takes a look out the window and then yells incredulously.

PETERSON:

We're *clear!*

Weinberg looks foolishly happy and then his knees buckle and he slides down beside Winocki, but no one notices him for they are tasting life again.

87. INT. COCKPIT QUINCANNON AND WILLIAMS

are tasting life, too. White stands rigidly behind them, gripping the chairs.

QUINCANNON:

Check fuel tanks. See if any of 'em are punctured. (White nods and exits aft swiftly. Irish switches on radio.) Zero five five six four to Hickam radio control. Zero five five six four to Hickam radio control.

RADIO:

Hickam tower to zero five five six four. Go ahead.

QUINCANNON:

Coming in for a landing. Is the field lit up?

RADIO:

It's lit up from here to Pearl Harbor. Stay where you are. Don't get off the ground.

QUINCANNON:

Sorry. Already off. I can see your beacon.

RADIO:

That's no beacon. It's the whole world on fire.

88. INT. RADIO SECTION

Weinberg is sitting on the floor watching with almost scientific interest the inert sprawled figure of Winocki. Sergeant White enters from forward, checking a fuel line with a flashlight. Weinberg looks up at him admiringly.

WEINBERG:

Boy, you sure got a wallop.

WHITE (gruffly):

It was a pleasure.

He notes Winocki is stirring and he stoops down over him. As Winocki opens his eyes, White and Weinberg help him up in a sitting position. He leans back against the bulkhead and looks around dizzily. His hand goes to his chin and it all comes clear as he looks up at White accusingly.

WHITE:

Listen, Winocki, we know you got guts—but you got to use your head, too. If it had been daylight we'd have cleaned out those snipers, but in the dark—well, Quincannon used his head. So stop tryin' to prove something.

WINOCKI (rubs his chin and looks him straight in the eye):

My job is tail gunner. What's yours—lecturing?

WHITE:

If that's the way you feel about it— (Straightens up and goes on with his work.)

Winocki's gaze follows White as he exits aft. Weinberg looks at Winocki with a glimmer in his eyes.

WEINBERG:

Say, don't you know dis is all just a drill?

Winocki stares at him but says nothing.

LAP DISSOLVE:

89. THE FORTRESS ROARING THROUGH THE NIGHT AT LOW ALTITUDE (MINIATURE)
First she is just a shape in darkness and then she is caught in a flicker of light from below, which licks over her in murky waves, leaving her topside dark.

90. INT. COCKPIT
The fiery light comes through the windows on the tense faces of Irish and Williams. Williams indicates down ahead and Irish nods grimly.

91–92. INCLUDED IN FOREGOING

93. INT. MEAT CAN
McMartin is crouched in the nose, outlined black against the increasing glare. Calls to Hauser at desk behind him.

McMARTIN:

For Pete's sake—look at Pearl Harbor!

Hauser slides in beside him, both silhouetted now.

94. SHOOTING DOWN PAST THEIR HEADS
Through the Plexiglas nose we see a ghastly inferno (miniature). Great fires are gushing up into a sky overhung with rolling smoke. At one side a battleship lies half on her side, burning fiercely, blotted out momentarily by heavy black smoke. Oil stores send up great tongues of flame. Further inland are other fires.

95. REVERSE CLOSE INTO AWED FACES OF McMARTIN AND HAUSER
lighted by the growing glare.

96. INT. COCKPIT

White behind the pilots, their faces lighted by the fires as they look down. The flickering light is bright on the ceiling over their heads.

QUINCANNON:

Pilot to crew. Take a good look at it, fellows—something to remember.

WHITE (looking down grimly):

Mary Ann won't forget it.

97. INT. RADIO SECTION

The faces of Peterson and the kid, lighted by the glare through window from below, tighten as they watch.

98. INT. WAIST SECTION

Faces of Weinberg and Winocki looking down, caught in the flickering light. Now Winocki has found something real to direct his embittered feelings against and his eyes grow hard and his jaw clenches.

LAP:

99. HICKAM FIELD LONG SHOT SHOOTING UP PAST SIDE OF BURNING HANGAR NIGHT

We hear a roar of engines and see the big airplane coming down through smoke and glare. Then she levels out along runway.

100. PAN SHOT

as her wheels touch and she bounces and bumps along the shell-pitted field and finally stops, silhouetted against fires in the distance. Dark figures of men dash out toward her.

101. INT. COCKPIT

Glare of burning hangar floods through windows on their faces as White, who has been tensely gripping the chair backs, lets go and starts aft hurriedly. Quincannon cuts the throttles to mere idling and leans back and lets out his breath as Williams with a nervous grin gives him the high sign of approval.

WILLIAMS:

How'd you miss those bomb craters?

QUINCANNON (grins sweatily as he indicates swinging toy):

I guess the kid was pulling for us.

102. GROUND FULL SHOT MARY ANN

bright in the glare as ground crew men come running in. The door opens and the crew piles out. The men make way for a tired-looking colonel who comes striding in toward ship accompanied by a sergeant.

103. NEAR SHOT GROUP AT DOOR

The crew are already on the ground, including Hauser and McMartin, as Quincannon jumps down followed by Williams. The colonel and sergeant stride into scene. Camera moves in.

COLONEL (offers hand):

Fine job, Captain—but you shouldn't have come.

QUINCANNON:

Had to, sir. We were getting shot at by a squad of snipers. Couldn't fight 'em in the dark, and I was afraid they'd hit a fuel tank.

COLONEL:

Mmmm, I see. We had plenty of trouble here too with the *friendly* Japanese. (Grimly.) Three trucks arrived from Honolulu at seven-thirty this morning—delivering supplies. When the first Jap plane showed up they slammed across the field and wrecked every airplane in sight. Cut the tails off all but three of our fighters.

WHITE (growls under his breath):
The sons of heaven!

WILLIAMS:
I hope we can get a crack at 'em, sir.

COLONEL:
You will. Which one of you is McMartin?

McMARTIN:
Me, sir.

COLONEL:
Well, now you're here, you'd better get over to the hospital.

McMARTIN:
My *sister?*

COLONEL (turns to sergeant as if he hadn't heard):
Sergeant, take them over in a jeep.

SERGEANT:
Yes, sir.

WILLIAMS (no less alarmed):
May I go along, sir?

COLONEL (nods):
You'd better go too, Quincannon.

QUINCANNON:
Yes, sir.

COLONEL (to White):
Stay with your airplane, sergeant. Get her serviced. Full fuel load. Full ammunition for the guns. Any repairs needed?

WHITE (his face sweating):
I can take care of 'em, sir. Excuse me, Colonel—but did they attack Clark Field at Manila?

COLONEL (nods):

We don't know how badly yet. They've hit everything in the Pacific—Guam, Wake, Midway— (His eyes harden.) and we're *still* not at war. (To the sergeant who waits for the trio.) Go along, Sergeant.

He turns away as Quincannon, Williams, and McMartin exit hurriedly after the sergeant. Camera moves in on White's face, and we see his anxiety about his son. Then he snaps out of it, half dead with weariness as he is.

WHITE:

Come on, you boys—look alive! We got work to do!

LAP DISSOLVE TO:

104. INT. CORRIDOR OF HOSPITAL

Shooting toward door we see the sergeant enter and motion McMartin, Williams, and Quincannon to follow him. As they step in hesitantly they look with shocked eyes at:

105. SHOOTING PAST THEM

We see the corridor wall is lined with army cots, all occupied by wounded and dying civilians. Nurses, some of them volunteers without uniforms, are busy with the groaning people. Camera trucks along on the sergeant and the three officers so that we glimpse the cots along the wall, most of them occupied by wounded women and children. One woman is propped up, a bandage tight across her upper face and eyes, holding a wailing baby tightly against her breast. In another cot a small Hawaiian boy of six, only his scared brown face showing above the sheet, is crying out to a nurse who grips his hand, trying to comfort him.

BOY:

My legs, nurse! Where's my *legs?*

NURSE (crying herself, as she puts her arms around the terrified child):

Hush, Jimmy. You're going to be all right.

BOY (almost hysterically):

But my *legs*—

Quickly our trio has passed on. At another cot we see a Chinese woman on her knees beside a cot where a young man lies still and white. She is bowing and in her throat making the age-old cry of women sorrowing for their dead. A nurse tries to get her to her feet. Now we have trucked our trio to the door at other end of the short corridor, and the sergeant beckons them through.

106. INT. SMALL ANTEROOM

The sergeant enters with the trio and halts, indicating a door at other side of room.

SERGEANT:

In there, sir.

McMartin swiftly opens the door and camera follows him, Williams, and Quincannon into the room. As they halt we see a nurse straighten up and make a warning gesture.

NURSE (whispers):

Only a moment, please. She must rest.

107. CLOSE SHOT IN FACES OF THE THREE BOYS

as they look at:

107A. CLOSE SHOT SUSAN'S PALE FACE

her hair spread out on the pillow. She smiles weakly.

SUSAN:

Hello, kids.

108. CLOSE GROUP SHOT

Williams almost groans.

WILLIAMS:
Susan!

McMARTIN (mutters shakily):
Sue-girl . . . Gee, Susan!

SUSAN:
Don't worry. I'm just taking a rest cure. (Her eyes glimmer.) Us McMartins are tough. I like to have people make a fuss over me. (Sighs weakly.) My, it's good to see you boys. (The talking has spent her strength and she closes her eyes for a moment. The nurse motions them to leave.) Tommy!

McMARTIN:
Yes, Sue?

SUSAN (drowsily):
I wanted to—tell you something—but—I'm so tired.

WILLIAMS (anxiously):
Not now, Susan.

McMARTIN:
We'll come back later.

SUSAN (persistently):
Just don't get mad at him. It was all my fault . . . He tried to make me get out of the car.

McMARTIN:
What car?

WILLIAMS:
Who?

SUSAN (faintly):
Tex Rader.

She lapses into silence as McMartin and Williams react. The nurse stoops and looks at her and then straightens up and motions to the boys as she whispers.

NURSE:

Come back in the morning. She needs rest.

Williams and McMartin stand rooted to the spot. Quincannon opens door softly and motions to them, and they follow him out bewilderedly.

LAP DISSOLVE TO:

109. INT. A HANGAR AT HICKAM FIELD (STUDIO)

Shooting toward the open door we see the figures of Williams, McMartin, and Quincannon outlined against the glare of distant fires as they enter the hangar. Williams switches on a flashlight and throws it around in the dark interior. Then he discovers what he is looking for and moves right. Camera pans on them.

110. MED. SHOT AN ARMY COT

The three enter scene and Williams throws the hard cone of light on an officer stretched out dead asleep on the cot. McMartin shakes his shoulder and the officer rouses and sits up, blinking in the harsh light. He is a tall, good-looking young fellow, but looks completely used up.

WILLIAMS:

Hello, Rader.

TEX (peers):

Oh—Williams. (Blinks tiredly.) Hello, Tommy. How're you, Quincannon? I've been waiting for you. Guess I went to sleep.

WILLIAMS (in a hard voice):

We've just come from the hospital.

TEX (anxiously):

How is she?

McMARTIN:

That's what we want to talk to you about.

WILLIAMS:

What'd she mean—talking about a car?

McMARTIN:

Yeah—*what?*

TEX (looks at them curiously):

What is this—the third degree?

QUINCANNON:

Go easy, fellows. She said it wasn't his fault.

TEX:

Don't believe what she said. It *was* my fault. I should have pitched her out of the car.

McMARTIN:

What car?

TEX:

One I borrowed for the beach party—

WILLIAMS:

What beach party?

QUINCANNON:

Listen. Given him a chance.

TEX:

We were just starting out when the first planes came over. I couldn't figure it out at first—I'd seen the dawn patrol come in—

McMARTIN:

Up early, weren't you?

WILLIAMS:

Or out late.

QUINCANNON:

Listen.

TEX:

I guess both of us spotted the Rising Sun on the

wings at the same time—and about that moment we heard the bombs.

McMARTIN:

Go on.

TEX:

All I could think of at that moment was how I could get to the field. I'd swung the car around. I told Susan to hop out and get under cover, but she only laughed at me—you know how she is.

WILLIAMS:

Go on.

TEX:

When we got near the field a big truck slowed itself across the road ahead of me and I saw I couldn't make it and jammed on the brakes. I could see it was a delivery truck from Honolulu and I remember thinking as I jumped out that the driver'd been hit. (Miserably.) I was pretty dumb, I guess. First thing I knew I heard an explosion right in my face and I realized the Jap behind the wheel had blazed away with a shotgun point blank—but a rotten shot. (His hand moves past his ear.) I sloughed him over the head with his own gun and got that truck off the road . . . I don't remember how. Other cars were coming along the road now, fellows trying to get there like me.

McMARTIN:

Was Susan all right?

TEX (nods):

That's when I should have thrown her out. She'd got behind the wheel and the minute I jumped in she was off like a shot. Right across the field to the hangar line, driving like she was crazy and me hanging on. Last I saw of her she was standing in that car, yelling and rooting for our boys like it was a football game.

WILLIAMS (tensely):
What happened to her?

TEX:
Machine-gunned. (There is a heavy silence as they look at him.) The soldier who ran out of his hangar to drag her in was killed.

McMARTIN:
What did you do?

TEX (as the sergeant who took them to the hospital enters):
What could I do?

SERGEANT (salutes Quincannon):
Excuse me, sir—the CO wants you.

QUINCANNON:
Where is he?

SERGEANT (indicates hangar line):
At your airplane, sir.

QUINCANNON (decently to Tex as he exits):
See you later, Rader. (Tex looks at Williams and McMartin.)

TEX:
I hope you fellows don't—

But he breaks off, for they turn abruptly with stony faces and exit after Quincannon. Rader sits on the cot looking after them thoughtfully.

111. FIELD OUTSIDE HANGAR WIDE ANGLE ON MARY ANN
A busy scene. Fuel truck pulling away. Men wheeling servicing gear under wings. Weinberg still working on one engine. The CO stands under the edge of one wing talking with Hauser, who has a case of charts under his arm, as Quincannon walks out to join them, followed by Williams and McMartin.

112. MED. SHOT ON CO AND HAUSER
as Quincannon and the others enter.

COLONEL:
How's your sister, McMartin?

McMARTIN (soberly):
Pretty weak, sir. The surgeon says it's hard to tell yet. I'll run over again in the morning.

COLONEL:
I'm afraid you won't. (They all look at him.) We want this airplane out of here before daylight and the possibility of any more raids.

QUINCANNON (dismayed):
You're sending us back to the *mainland*, sir?

COLONEL:
No—to Manila. You said you wanted a crack at the Japs. Well, here's your chance. (They look at him flabbergasted.) I know you're all tired and I know it's a hazardous flight. But we think we're safe here for the moment and the Philippines are in bad shape. My orders are to send 'em as many B-17s as we can. (Eyes Quincannon challengingly.) Think you can make it?

QUINCANNON:
Where can we pick up more fuel, sir?

COLONEL:
Wake Island—I hope. We've still got Midway but it's off your route. Guam may have fallen—we don't know. I can't promise you how long Wake will hold out or what you'll find when you get there.

QUINCANNON (turns to Hauser):
Better pick up the charts right away, Monk.

HAUSER (grins and pats his case):
I've already got 'em.

QUINCANNON (gives him a look as if to say "So you knew, you so-and-so!"; turns and calls off):

Sergeant White!

WHITE (entering):

Yes, sir?

QUINCANNON:

How's she running?

WHITE (wipes sweat from his face with the back of a greasy hand):

Number three engine's a little rough, sir. The men are too tired to work on it now—we can overhaul it in the morning.

QUINCANNON:

We're taking off in two hours.

WHITE (blinks):

Sir?

QUINCANNON:

I think you're going to see that son of yours, chief.

WHITE:

Manila?

QUINCANNON:

Why not? Can't you get that engine going right?

WHITE:

You bet I can, sir. I'll have her knockin' home runs in ninety minutes flat.

QUINCANNON:

Hop to it. Tell the crew they can sleep in the next world.

CO (as White exits briskly):

I've got to see the General—but I'll be back before takeoff. (Starts, then stops.) Oh, yes—tell your passenger I'll have some papers for him to deliver to Clark Field.

QUINCANNON:

What passenger, sir?

CO:

Didn't he report yet? (Quincannon shakes head.) Manila needs pilots. We've got more pursuit pilots here than planes right now and I'm sending one along with you.

QUINCANNON:

Who, sir?

CO:

I think you know him. He was at March Field with you last year. Lieutenant Rader.

WILLIAMS (blurts out):

Tex Rader?

CO (mistaking that blurt for eager friendship):

That's him. (Warmly.) Good man, Rader. Only three of our fighters got off the ground this morning and he was one of 'em. Knocked off four Jap Zeros before they shot him down. I've recommended him for a DFC. (They are silent because they are speechless but the CO doesn't know this.) Guess he's grabbing some sleep. Can't blame him for being fagged out after a day like that. See you later.

He strides off as Williams and McMartin look at each other, stunned. Quincannon grins at them.

QUINCANNON:

Shall I dust off a spot on the ground, boys—or don't you mind where you fall?

DISSOLVE:

113. FIELD FULL SHOT MARY ANN

has four great engines roaring as she starts down the runway. Camera pans on her as she lifts into the night and heads toward the setting moon, into the unpredictable perils of the far Pacific.

FADE OUT

FADE IN

114. LONG SHOT FLYING FORTRESS NIGHT
from camera plane. (About 4 A.M.)

115. NEAR SHOT
to make out her name.

LAP DISSOLVE TO:

116–17. OMITTED

118. INSERT CHART
Pencil draws a thin line to a tiny dot.

119. CLOSE TWO-SHOT
Weinberg watching as Hauser finishes and lays down pencil, working over his chart. Weinberg has brought him coffee. McMartin lies asleep on floor nearby.

WEINBERG (uneasily):
Is *dat* Wake Island?

HAUSER (working):
Not very big, is it?

WEINBERG:
Like tryin' to find a buckshot in the middle of Central Park. (Leans over confidentially.) How we doin', sir?

HAUSER (looks up with good-humored impatience):
You're the fifth guy who's been down here worrying. Why don't you get some sleep?

WEINBERG (hurriedly):
Yes, sir—I was just askin', sir.

120. INT. RADIO SECTION
The kid on watch, yawning a bit as White comes through on his way aft. Looks at the kid, pats him on shoulder as he passes.

121. INT. WAISTSECTION

Tex Rader sits apart and alone, the only one awake in the compartment. Winocki and Peterson sprawled asleep. White comes in and stoops and shakes Peterson.

WHITE:

Time to relieve the kid, Minnesota. (Looks at Rader as Peterson gets up sleepily.) Want anything, Lieutenant?

TEX:

No thanks, Sergeant. I want to get out of this flying boxcar, but I guess I can wait till we get to Manila.

WHITE (looks him straight in the eye):

If you mean *this airplane*, sir, her name is Mary Ann.

TEX (nods good-humoredly):

Yeah, I know.

WHITE:

There isn't a better airplane in the Army.

TEX (deliberately getting a rise):

Oh, if you're talking about bombers.

WHITE:

Any airplanes, sir.

TEX:

I'll stick to the pursuit ships, Sergeant.

White exits stiffly and Tex looks after him with amusement.

122. INT. COCKPIT

Quincannon and Williams tired and silent as White comes in and leans behind them.

QUINCANNON:

Why don't you get some sleep, Robbie?

WHITE:

Going to, sir. (Growls.) These pursuit pilots—they get my goat.

WILLIAMS:

Mine, too. Especially if you're talking about that one back there in the tail.

WHITE (still burning):

The only time we ever had any trouble with a B-17 was when he flew into us at March Field with that cockeyed P-40.

WILLIAMS:

Yeah—trying to make a grandstand landing.

QUINCANNON:

Better turn in, chief. Soon be daylight.

WHITE:

Yes, sir. (Turns away and crawls down hatch into meat can.)

123–26. OMITTED

127. INT. MEAT CAN

Hauser busy over chart as White comes to desk with pretended casualness.

WHITE:

How we doing, sir?

HAUSER (rears up at him):

Say, don't you fellows ever sleep? Every fifteen minutes somebody wakes up and comes down here to find out if I know *where* we are or if I'm going to get this airplane lost. (Then ruefully.) Oh, I'm sorry, Robbie, I guess I'm just on edge.

WHITE (grins as he points at the photo):

That's just the way your old man would've told me

off—only he'd have done it with a four-star cussing. Now tell me—*how are we doing?*

HAUSER (has to laugh):
We're doing all right, you pest. I think we're gonna hit Wake island right on the nose—with two hours fuel to spare.

WHITE (pats him on the back):
Thanks. Now I can hit the hay.

LAP DISSOLVE TO:

128. LONG SHOT MARY ANN FROM CAMERA PLANE DAY
The rising sun sparkling on clouds astern of her.

LAP DISSOLVE TO:

129. OMITTED

130. INT. COCKPIT
Quincannon and Williams flying the ship as McMartin comes in like a gust of wind, waving the radiogram.

McMARTIN:
Great news, Bill! (To Quincannon, who looks inquiringly at Williams, who is glancing at the message.) It's about Susan—just got it on the radio. Mighty fine of the CO to think of that.

QUINCANNON (impatiently):
Well, what's it *say?*

WILLIAMS (elatedly):
She's going to be okay!

McMARTIN (to Quincannon, who takes the message from Williams):
The head surgeon says she'll be on her way back to the States in three–four weeks.

WILLIAMS:
Gee, that's great.

McMARTIN (elatedly):
I'll say it is!

QUINCANNON (grins at them):
It certainly makes a change in you two.

McMARTIN (grinning happily):
You don't look so blue yourself.

QUINCANNON (hands him the message):
Better show it to our passenger. The poor guy is worrying.

WILLIAMS:
Let 'im worry. He's got it coming to him.

QUINCANNON:
Don't you think you fellows are being a little too rough with Rader?

WILLIAMS:
I haven't kicked him in the face yet, have I?

QUINCANNON:
I'm serious. You don't want to be unfair— You know it wasn't his fault—what happened to Susan.

McMARTIN:
That's right, Bill.

WILLIAMS:
Sure, it's right—I don't hold that against him.

McMARTIN:
Neither do I.

QUINCANNON:
I knew you'd feel that way. The poor guy had tough luck— He felt just as sick about it as we did.

WILLIAMS:
Yeah, but what was he doing out with Susan in the first place?

QUINCANNON (softly):

Say, are you jealous?

WILLIAMS:

Well—maybe I am. (A little ashamed of himself, he switches on interphone.) Peterson . . . Ask Lieutenant Rader to come up here.

PETERSON'S VOICE:

Yes, sir.

QUINCANNON:

That's the stuff. This is no time for hard feelings. We've had our trouble with him—but we all know he's okay—and a good pilot. (Williams seems to dissent at that last.) He was all right at Hickam Field, wasn't he?

WILLIAMS (nods):

But he's been shooting off his face against big airplanes ever since they gave him a pair of wings and a pursuit job.

QUINCANNON:

That's the trouble—he doesn't know any better. He's just grown up in those peashooters. Give 'im a break.

Makes a warning sign to them as he sees Rader coming along catwalk. They are all innocently watching out as Tex comes in, quite at ease.

TEX:

Want to see me, Williams?

McMARTIN:

Take a look at this.

Tex takes the radiogram and his face lights up, too, forgetting all about their antagonism in his glad reaction.

TEX:

Say, that's fine! (Looks at them soberly.) I'm mighty glad, fellows. That takes a big load off my mind.

WILLIAMS (embarrassed):

You know, Tex, we were—uh—all pretty upset last night. If we said anything out of line—

TEX (warmly):

Forget it. We were all on edge. I know *I* was.

WILLIAMS (gruffly):

Mighty decent of you to take it that way.

TEX:

Not a bit. I know how you felt. I don't blame you.

McMARTIN:

Thanks, Tex. After all, we've known each other a long time. (Sheepishly.) Had our little arguments about *Mary Ann* and your peashooters.

TEX:

Forget it, Tommy. Just a matter of opinion.

QUINCANNON (with a note of pride):

Not a bad airplane after all, is she?

TEX (grins):

I'm a passenger now. I can't complain.

130A. INT. MEAT CAN

Hauser has worked out a fix. Cuts in on interphone.

HAUSER:

Navigator to pilot—

QUINCANNON'S VOICE:

Go ahead, Monk.

HAUSER:

Just checking on drift. I underestimated a bit. Correct course two degrees to two twenty-four.

130B. INT. COCKPIT
Quincannon on interphone.

QUINCANNON:
Two two four she is.

Reaches over and sets:

130C. INSERT AUTOMATIC FLIGHT CONTROL DEVICE
as he sets course to 224.

130D. THREE-SHOT
Tex has leaned over to watch the adjustment. Quincannon as peacemaker notes his interest and explains.

QUINCANNON:
That's the new automatic flight control.

TEX:
I know the old type AFCD.

QUINCANNON (smiles):
It's about time you found out what the B-17s will do. Want to fly her?

TEX (points at AFCD):
Looks to me like she's flying herself.

QUINCANNON (proud):
She is right now.

TEX:
The man that counts now is the navigator. (Indicates AFCD, to McMartin.) Pretty smart gadget, Tommy. Almost as slick as your bombsight.

McMARTIN (his pride touched):
Not quite, Tex. We call that the one-ton brain.

TEX (nods):
How about this AFCD? Isn't it a mechanical brain, too?

QUINCANNON (pleased to educate Tex so rapidly):
Does everything but think.

TEX (looks at him innocently):
It's doing the thinking *now*, isn't it?

WILLIAMS (narrowly watching Tex):
Watch out for him, Irish.

TEX:
What's the matter with you, Williams—did you hear about it, too?

WILLIAMS (suspiciously):
Hear *what?*

TEX (very seriously):
Why in the next war they're going to give commissions to these mechanical brains in the bombers—yeah, put 'em in uniform and teach 'em to talk—and let Douglas turn out bomber pilots on the assembly line.

WILLIAMS (explodes):
Get him outa here, Tommy!

TEX (acts it out, pressing imaginary levers and pushing buttons):
We pursuit pilots will be upstairs fighting and we'll look down and see a flock of these mechanized freight trains coming along. Press a button—"Lieutenant AFCD?" "Yes, sir," says that thing. "Drop another load of potatoes on the enemy." (Salutes himself.) "Yes, sir. I'll tell Captain Bombsight right away, sir." "Very well,'" I say. "Where's your pilots?" "We left 'em on the ground, sir—we don't need 'em anymore and their heads take up so much room, sir."

WILLIAMS (blasts):
Get him outa this cockpit, Tommy, before I crown 'im!

TEX (politely):

What's the matter, Williams? I wouldn't say anything against these big bombers—they're fine for carrying passengers—but I wouldn't want to *fight* in one.

WILLIAMS:

You'll never get a *chance!*

TEX:

In a pursuit ship you're a one-man army, not a taxi driver. You're on your own—you don't have to wait for orders from a guy who can't fly they call a bombardier.

McMARTIN (the peacemaker blows up with a loud bang):

Hey—wait a minute!

TEX (innocently):

You know you give orders to these taxi drivers, Tommy, when you go to lay eggs. "Where to, sir?" says the Irishman. And you say, "Oh, go on a few blocks more and turn right. And give me change for a nickel, conductor."

WILLIAMS:

Will you get outa here?

TEX (goes right on):

And then when you get to Thirty-third Street and Broadway you throw an egg out the window—and run. *Very* exciting! I wouldn't fly this crate if they made me a brigadier for it!

WILLIAMS (rears out of his seat):

Listen, you egg-headed—

QUINCANNON (cuts in sharply):

Bill! Pipe down! Shut up, Rader! (On interphone.) Go ahead, Peterson. What is it?

131. INT. RADIO SECTION

Weinberg, Winocki, White, and the kid are crowded around Peterson.

PETERSON (on interphone):

I've picked up Washington on the shortwave, sir. The president's coming on.

132. INT. COCKPIT

The battle is suspended as they look at Quincannon.

QUINCANNON (on interphone):

Thanks. (To McMartin.) Washington on shortwave! Get back there and grab yourself some headphones. Take the gentleman with you.

McMARTIN (looks at Tex):

Do I *have* to?

QUINCANNON:

Take him!

Tex smiles at last as he follows McMartin aft.

133. INT. RADIO SECTION

White, Winocki, Weinberg, and the kid gathered around, having plugged in extra headphones as Peterson adjusts dials and brings up volume. Through static and fragments of voices we suddenly hear the voice of the Speaker of the House. (Tommy and Tex come in and get phones on during first few lines.)

SPEAKER:

Ladies and gentlemen, the president of the United States! (Applause and then all noise dies out as President Roosevelt's voice comes in strongly.)

PRESIDENT:

Yesterday, December seventh, 1941— a date which will live in infamy—the United States of America was suddenly and deliberately attacked by naval and air forces of the Empire of Japan.

134. INT. COCKPIT CLOSE ON FACES
of Quincannon and Williams, as voice continues.

PRESIDENT:

The attack yesterday on the Hawaiian Islands has caused severe damage to the American naval and military forces.

135. INT. MEAT CAN CLOSE ON HAUSER'S FACE
as he listens, forgetting his charts.

PRESIDENT:

Very many American lives have been lost. Always will our nation remember the character of the onslaught against us. (Sound of a roar like a cry of vengeance from the assembled Senate.)

136. INT. RADIO SECTION
First a group shot, all listening tensely, no man stirring, and then successive close-ups for reactions as voice continues:

PRESIDENT:

No matter how long it may take us to overcome this premeditated invasion the American people in their righteous might will win through to absolute victory. (Another cheering roar.) We will not only defend ourselves to the uttermost but will make it very certain that this form of treachery shall never again endanger us. We will gain the inevitable triumph—so help us God. I ask that Congress declare a state of war.

Over the roar that ensues we hear a clamor of voices.

VOICES:

Vote! Vote! Vote! (Speaker's gavel pounding for order over uproar.)

137. CLOSE GROUP SHOT THE MEN
unstirring as they listen. Weinberg shouts excitedly to White over the din.

WEINBERG:

Why dey have to vote? Don't dey know we're *already in it?*

WHITE (as Peterson tunes down the continuing roar and shouts for "vote"):

Listen, any buck-toothed little runt can walk up behind Joe Louis and knock him cold with a baseball bat—but a clean man don't do it. Your Uncle Sammy is civilized: He says, "Look out, you sneaks, we're gonna hit above the belt and knock the daylights outa you!"

WEINBERG:

Well, Weinberg is waitin'. (Yells at radio.) Ring dat bell, Congress!

138. CLOSE ON TOMMY AND TEX

listening as the clamor of voices comes full volume again and we hear the shouted refrain: "Vote! Vote! Vote!" Their faces are stern. Then they look at each other and Tommy sticks out his hand. Tex smiles as they grip.

DISSOLVE TO:

139–40. MARY ANN (FROM CAMERA PLANE) NIGHT

flying over the moonlit lonely sea.

141. INT. COCKPIT

Quincannon flying while Williams watches ahead anxiously.

142. SHOT THROUGH PLEXIGLAS NOSE

into faces of McMartin and Hauser watching ahead with worried faces.

143. INT. DOOR SECTION WEINBERG, RADER, WINOCKI, PETERSON

sitting around as if waiting for a streetcar, no one speaking. White comes through aft and they watch him but he says nothing.

144. INT. RADIO SECTION THE KID
at radio desk as White enters and leans over, voice low.

WHITE:
Pick up Wake Island?

The kid looks up and shakes his head and White goes forward.

145. INT. COCKPIT
Quincannon looks at Williams, who shakes his head and goes on staring ahead. White enters as Quincannon switches to interphone.

QUINCANNON:
See anything, Tommy?

McMARTIN'S VOICE:
Not yet.

QUINCANNON:
What do you think, Monk?

146. INT. MEAT CAN
Hauser is back at his navigator's desk. Picks up mikes, a little worried but hiding it.

HAUSER:
We ought to be over in twenty minutes, skipper. If we don't see anything, better turn right.

QUINCANNON'S VOICE (laconically):
Okay.

McMARTIN'S VOICE (sharply from nose):
Monk!

Hauser jumps up and goes to—

147. SHOT (THROUGH PLEXIGLAS NOSE)
on their faces as Hauser slides in beside him. Their faces react as Tommy points.

148. REVERSE SHOOTING PAST THEIR HEADS

We see through the glass nose a tiny fiery beacon breaking through a cloud. Tommy sings out on interphone.

McMARTIN:

There she is, Irish! Dead ahead! (And he begins thumping Hauser on the back.)

149. INT. COCKPIT INTO FACES OF QUINCANNON AND WILLIAMS

as they sight it too. Reactions as Quincannon touches the toy elephant and switches on interphone.

QUINCANNON:

Pilot to crew! Wake Island ahead! Looks like it's on fire!

150. INT. DOOR SECTION

All the men are jumping up excitedly and trying to get a glimpse through the side windows. Weinberg yells out:

WEINBERG:

T'ree cheers for duh navigator!

DISSOLVE TO:

151. WAKE ISLAND LANDING FIELD SHOOTING PAST EDGE

of a burning machine shop we hear the deep roar of the incoming four-engined bomber, and then through rolling smoke we see the big ship nose down and make a landing on the lurid shell-pitted strip.

LAP DISSOLVE TO:

152. NEAR SHOT AT DOOR OF MARY ANN

The marine officer in command, Major Daniels, strides in as Quincannon jumps down. Flamelight on them.

MAJOR DANIELS:

Good work, Captain! (Grips hands.) Major Daniels, in command.

QUINCANNON:

Quincannon. Thank you, sir. (Grins as others are climbing out.) This is our navigator—Lieutenant Hauser. We're going to put him in a glass case in a museum. (Others.) Lieutenants Williams, McMartin, Rader!

DANIELS (shaking hands):

Good thing you weren't here Monday. Sixty Jap bombers gave us a surprise party.

TEX:

You mean Sunday, don't you, sir?

DANIELS (shakes head):

Monday here was Sunday in Honolulu. You've crossed the date line.

QUINCANNON:

He's a pursuit pilot, Major. They don't know much about geography. (Daniels grins.) Can our men bunk down somewhere for five or six hours? They're all in.

DANIELS (looks at him):

In six hours you'd better be five and a half hours out. (Nods at fires.) With these beacons the Jap doesn't have to wait for daylight to come calling. My orders are to get you out of here in twenty minutes.

For a moment the crew members who have gathered around the officers just stand silent. Quincannon turns to Sergeant White.

QUINCANNON:

Can you get her refueled and ready?

WHITE:

Yes, sir.

DANIELS:

Our air force commander wants to see you, Quincannon. Major Bagley.

Quincannon follows him out and his officers follow.

153. FULL SHOT MARY ANN

Members of the marine ground crew are moving in with fuel truck and servicing equipment. They begin switching on hand lights to work by. Sergeant White takes charge.

LAP DISSOLVE TO:

154. INT. HOSPITAL GROUP SHOT

Just a corner of a wrecked ward. Plaster off walls, ceiling gaping overhead, fires visible through one window and perhaps we can see the fortress and the men working swiftly around it. Daniels, Quincannon, Rader, Hauser, McMartin, and Williams are gathered around a cot on which lies a severely wounded, bandaged yet cheerful man—Major Bagley. The young men stand erect and respectful. Bagley has questioned them and his eyes are very stern as he looks at Quincannon.

BAGLEY:

So they really got the *Arizona?*

QUINCANNON:

Yes, sir. Hickam Field was smashed just as bad as Pearl Harbor. Lot of fifth column work.

TEX (as Bagley compresses his lips):

None of our bombers got off the ground, sir.

BAGLEY (his eyes are bitter):

Same thing here. If we'd had our twelve fighters up, we'd have smeared them on that first attack. But we were listening on the shortwave to Tokyo telling about Mr. Saburo Kurusu's peace mission to the United States. (Quietly.) I've studied all the wars of history, gentlemen, but I've never come across any treachery to match that.

QUINCANNON:

How many airplanes have you got, sir?

BAGLEY:

A week ago we didn't have any. Few days ago they flew in twelve fighters from one of our carriers. (Sighs.) Eight were destroyed on the ground, after they'd come in from dawn patrol.

TEX (aghast):

Only four left, sir?

BAGLEY (shakes head):

Two—and one won't fly. Those four P-40s took on sixty Nippos this afternoon. Shot down plenty of 'em but— (Wearily.) Hogan and Ingersoll died fighting. You knew them I think.

Tex nods bleakly.

QUINCANNON (beginning to realize how tough things are):

What will you do when they come back, Major?

BAGLEY (quietly):

We've got a lad out there getting a wink of sleep who will take 'em all on single-handed. Lieutenant Rose.

TEX (reacts):

Bertie Rose?

BAGLEY:

That's him.

TEX (flabbergasted):

You fellows remember Rosie at Randolph Field. Everyone kidded him on account of his size. About so high— (Indicates below his shoulder.)

WILLIAMS (equally astonished):

Sure. We know Rosie.

QUINCANNON:

Could we—uh—talk to him, sir, before we hop off?

TEX:

I'd like to stand up and salute him.

DANIELS (smiles as White enters and salutes Quincannon):

I'll tell him what you said, McMartin. He needs that sleep. May have to roust him out any minute and he's not been doing much sleeping lately.

WHITE (to Quincannon):

All ready, sir.

BAGLEY (puts out his hand to Quincannon wearily):

Well, good luck. It's done me good to see you fellows. Go out there and blast the Japs. Teach 'em treachery can't win—no matter how much head start it has.

DANIELS:

You young fellows have got to do it. *We* know we're only fighting a delaying action here.

QUINCANNON:

You . . . can't hold out, sir?

DANIELS (not admitting anything):

I've got four hundred marines and they're fighting mad. It's going to be a fine scrap.

He glances at Bagley's wearily closed eyes and makes a sign they'd better leave.

QUINCANNON:

Just one last question, sir— (To the man in bed.) Major Bagley— (Bagley opens his eyes.) Can't we fly you out? You and the rest of the wounded?

BAGLEY:

Thank you, I'm fine here. (Smiles thinly.) I'm not worth my weight in gasoline. Me nor anyone else.

That airplane of yours is needed in Manila. Get it there.

QUINCANNON (disappointed):
Yes, sir.

DANIELS (grins):
He wouldn't leave this island paradise if you offered him a lower berth in a Pullman—or a brigadier's star.

BAGLEY:
If you see my old commander, General MacArthur, tell him no matter what the news is that we're in here pitching till they strike us out.

QUINCANNON (gruffly):
We will, sir.

BAGLEY (cheerfully):
I'll be seeing you somewhere. All the luck.

Daniels motions them again as Bagley closes his eyes and they go out quietly. Sergeant White glances wonderingly at the man on the bed as he follows them very quietly.

155. FIELD FULL SHOT SHIP
Ground crew is pulling away its servicing equipment. A group of marines gathered near door with Weinberg, Winocki, and Peterson. The kid is under a wing, forward, talking with several face-stubbled dirty-uniformed marines.

156. CLOSE ON KID AND THE THREE MARINES
The kid has his hands full of letters and one of them hands him a couple more.

MARINE (grins):
One for the wife and one for the kid. He'll be old enough to read by the time I get back to the States.

SECOND MARINE:

Don't lose 'em, kid.

KID:

Don't worry— (Smiles.) Funny thing, I was going to leave a letter of my own here for the *Clipper.*

FIRST MARINE (grins):

She got outa here yesterday. Twenty-six bullet holes in 'er and her crew so mad they wanted to stay here and fight.

SECOND MARINE (laughs):

The old man had to get tough with 'em.

157. INCLUDED IN SCENE 154

158. FIELD GROUP AT DOOR OF MARY ANN

Weinberg, Winocki, Peterson, and the kid are facing several marines, their faces smoke-streaked and unshaven. One of them is trying to give Weinberg a nondescript little dog but Weinberg is protesting, glancing off uneasily to see if the officers are coming.

WEINBERG:

It's against duh regulations, pal. You don't wanta get me busted.

MARINE WITH DOG:

Come on, soldier. We don't want Tripoli to get hurt.

SECOND MARINE:

We give him the rank of top sergeant!

THIRD MARINE:

He ain't got no pedigree, but he sure can fight!

MARINE WITH DOG:

Say, he'd tackle a Jap three times his size!

WEINBERG:

I wisht I could but I can't. Get in a fine jam.

SECOND MARINE:

Turn him over to the marines at Manila. We got to git him outa here.

MARINE WITH DOG:

Look—he's trained. Hey, Tripoli—you like Mr. Moto? (Dog snarls fiercely.) See?

WEINBERG:

Ain't dat cute, Winocki?

WINOCKI:

Pretty smart all right.

MARINE WITH DOG (tries to give him dog):

Come on, soldier.

WEINBERG (shakes head):

Chee, I'd like to, honest, but— (Stops as the dog reaches out and licks his hand. He sighs and takes it in his arms.) Here goes me promotion.

WINOCKI (swiftly):

Duck. Here they come.

Weinberg hurriedly climbs into the airplane with the dog in his arms. The marines look after him with relief and pleasure as Quincannon enters with Major Daniels and the other four officers.

WHITE:

Come on, kid. Inside. (To Peterson.) Where's Weinberg?

PETERSON (as Winocki climbs in, followed by the kid with letters):

On board, chief.

WHITE:

Okay. Get in.

He climbs in after Peterson. Major Daniels is shaking hands with the officers and they climb in one after another, Williams, Hauser, McMartin, and Rader. Quincannon shakes hands last, almost hating to go.

QUINCANNON:
Goodbye, sir. And luck.

DANIELS (cheerfully):
Same to you boys.

QUINCANNON:
Anything we can do for you in Manila?

DANIELS (grins):
Send us some more Japs!

Quincannon can't help grinning at that indomitable spirit as he climbs in after Sergeant White.

LAP DISSOLVE TO:

159. SHOT PAST MAJOR DANIELS
standing alone on the field as the big airplane thunders away from him, caught in the lurid light from the burning machine shop, and takes the air.

160. CLOSE SHOT INTO DANIELS'S FACE
The flame light on it as his smile fades away and he lifts his hand in an unconscious salute of good luck. We hear the roar of the plane receding.

161. MARY ANN FROM CAMERA PLANE
as she levels off, her engines pulsing, gleaming in the moonlight as she heads into the perilous and unknown west for the last leg.

FADE OUT

FADE IN

162. LONG SHOT MARY ANN DAY
from camera plane.

LAP DISSOLVE TO:

163–64. INCLUDED IN FOLLOWING

165. INSERT CHART
Pencil draws line from Wake Island to Manila.

165A. CLOSE SHOT HAUSER
as he lays out course, marking position on the line.

QUINCANNON'S VOICE:
Pilot to navigator—

HAUSER:
Yeah?

QUINCANNON:
How're we doing, genius?

HAUSER:
About eleven hundred miles from Manila. I'll have the exact position worked out in a few minutes. We're bucking a thirty-knot wind.

166. INT. COCKPIT
Williams enters from aft and slides into his seat as Quincannon responds to Hauser.

QUINCANNON:
Don't I know it. Looks like we're going to get bounced around.

HAUSER'S VOICE:
Well, that's one way to keep awake.

WILLIAMS (peers ahead with eyes red-rimmed from lack of sleep):
What's that muck ahead?

QUINCANNON:
That's what I'm wondering. Looks like a storm front.

167. INT. RADIO SECTION
Weinberg sits on a parachute. Winocki in chair. Peterson is putting a new tube in the radio set. Weinberg has

been talking with Winocki to keep awake and now he looks at him with some astonishment as the ship hits a bump.

WEINBERG:

Chee, I didn't know dat, Joe. You played left tackle for Notre Dame? (Winocki nods, bored.) Chee, you must be smart—workin' your way t'rough college.

WINOCKI:

I've seen guys with college degrees didn't know enough to come in outa the rain. (Scowls.) It only meant one thing to me.

WEINBERG (deeply interested):

What's dat?

WINOCKI:

The way to get into an army flying school.

WEINBERG (shakes head):

Too bad you got busted out. Didn't you never even solo?

WINOCKI (aggressively):

Sure I soloed. I could fly one of these big crates if I'd been given a chance.[2]

168. INT. TAIL SECTION

Sergeant White and Tex Rader are stretched out getting a few winks of sleep. The ship hits another bump and White wakens.

169. CLOSE SHOT WHITE

as he sits up. Then as he happens to look past camera he reacts.

170. CLOSE SHOT WHAT HE SEES DUFFEL BAG

stowed with other luggage in narrow part of tail. The duffel bag seems to have come alive. Though it is tied loosely at the mouth it is moving about and trying to walk.

171. CLOSE SHOT WHITE
for startled reaction. He throws off the blanket and jumps up.

172. CLOSE SHOT DUFFEL BAG
as White pounces on it as if he feared it were a bomb. Jerks the cord loose from the mouth and Tripoli crawls out. White's face is a study. But the dog climbs on his knees and tries to lick his face and his angry eyes soften.

173. INT. RADIO SECTION
Weinberg has been discussing the kid anxiously as White bursts in from the after section with the dog under his arm. The three faces affect intense astonishment as White holds up the dog with righteous indignation.

WHITE:
Who belongs to this?

PETERSON (with innocent amazement):
Christmas crackers!

WEINBERG (uneasily):
Is dat your dog, chief?

WHITE (blows up):
No, it isn't my dog! What kind of a crew chief do you think I am? (Grimly to them all.) Who put it on this airplane?

WEINBERG (in the uneasy silence):
Maybe he jus' walked on.

WHITE (with fine wrath):
And tied hisself in a *sack?* (Weinberg draws back uneasily from Tripoli, who tries to lick his face.) Who did it? (Looks at Peterson sternly.) *You?* (Peterson doesn't know what to say but he shakes his head.) *Weinberg?*

WEINBERG (talking fast):

Maybe duh marines done it, Sergeant. Dey had a dog named Tripoli on Wake Island. He had a cute trick too. Let's see if dis is him. (Leans close to dog.) Looky here, Tripoli—whaddye think of Mr. Moto? (Dog snarls.) *Moto!* (Dog barks fiercely and Weinberg grins up at White but instantly wipes the grin off his face, seeing trouble.)

WHITE (grimly):

Did you bring this dog on board?

WINOCKI (before Weinberg can answer):

Why don't you ask me, Sergeant? (White turns on him.) Sure—I'm it! Go on, tell Quincannon. He busted me once—here's his chance to bust me again.

WEINBERG:

Listen, Joe—

WINOCKI:

Shut up!

WHITE (stares at Winocki sarcastically):

Very bright, Winocki. How'd you ever get those sergeant's stripes?

WINOCKI:

I got 'em for bein' dumb. Go ahead—report me.

WHITE (grimly):

Well, you're askin' for it.

WEINBERG (as White starts forward with dog under arm):

Wait a minute, chief—it was me.

White looks back at Weinberg disbelievingly, then goes forward.

WINOCKI:

Shut your trap!

WEINBERG (pays no attention, looking at White in doorway):

I done it an' I'll take duh rap. Lissen, you wouldn'ta left dat little pooch dere neither. You know what's gonna happen at Wake well as dey do— Dat's why dey asked me to take 'im.

White exits without a word and Weinberg looks defiantly at Winocki, who gives him a look as if to say, "You damned fool."

174–75. OMITTED

176. INT. COCKPIT

McMartin is leaning on the back of Quincannon's chair, and they are all watching the weather ahead anxiously as White enters behind them with the dog, which at that moment barks and they all jump and look around, flabbergasted.

QUINCANNON:

What is this, Robbie—Noah's ark?

WHITE:

Sorry, sir.

QUINCANNON (as Tommy rubs the dog's ears):

What'd he do—fly in the window?

WHITE:

One of the crew brought 'im on board, sir. (He waits for Irish to ask who, but Irish doesn't.)

McMARTIN (pets the tail-wagger):

Cute little pooch. Hiya, fella—your rudder's working all right.

WHITE:

Call 'im Tripoli. He don't like the Jap— (To dog.) You like that guy *Moto?* (Dog snarls and they grin.)

WILLIAMS (looks at Quincannon):
Tough spot for a dog if we have to climb over that stuff ahead.

QUINCANNON (indicates aft; to White):
Who back there likes dogs?

WHITE (seeing the point):
I think Winocki likes dogs.

QUINCANNON:
You think he'd like to take care of him?

WHITE:
I think he's just the man, sir.

QUINCANNON (the ship bounces and they all hang on):
Okay. He'll have to put 'im on oxygen if this storm front is as high as it looks.

White exits aft with Tripoli as the boys look at each other, amused by the sergeant's relief.

WILLIAMS:
Don't tell me Winocki has a sentimental heart. Now if he'd said *Weinberg*—

QUINCANNON:
Funny how a fellow will let on he's a tough nut—just because inside he's worried.

McMARTIN (sighs):
I wish it'd been Tex Rader. I'd love to see *that* bird feeding a dog oxygen from a bottle!

He starts aft and Williams, getting a nod from Irish, slides out of his seat and follows him for a stretch. Ship bouncing now.

177. INT. WAIST SECTION
Winocki, who has fixed himself a fresh seat, looks up defiantly as White enters with the dog, looking for him.

WINOCKI:

What's the sentence, judge?

WHITE (growls):

Never mind that now. (Drops dog in his lap.) It's your responsibility. Take care of him.

Winocki looks at him suspiciously as McMartin and Williams enter and light cigarettes. From the tail section enters Tex Rader, awakened by the ship's bouncing.

TEX:

If you miss any rivets out of that tail section you'll find 'em in my neck— (Stops short and stares at dog Winocki holds.) What *is* this—a flying doghouse?

McMARTIN:

Look out—he don't like pursuit pilots.

TEX:

What's his name?

McMARTIN:

Moto.

TEX (reaches out):

Hiya, Moto! (Dog snarls and he jerks back his hand.)

WILLIAMS:

Didn't we tell you?

McMARTIN:

That dog's a judge of character.

Tex looks at them suspiciously and then starts to pet the dog again but with a certain caution.

TEX:

Here, Moto. Nice, Moto— (Dog snarls so fiercely he jerks back his hand.) Hey, *Moto!*

The dog snaps at him and he backs off as Williams and McMartin grin blissfully and even White smiles discreetly.

WILLIAMS:

You better get out of here. If he gets loose—

The ship hits a very hard bump and they all hang on.

LAP DISSOLVE TO:

178. LONG SHOT OF THE FORTRESS

flying straight toward an awful mess of clouds that rises to an immense height. Still climbing.

179. INT. COCKPIT SHOOTING PAST PILOTS' HEADS

We see the dark mass of the storm front. Ship bumping heavily now. White enters from bomb bay, hanging on to whatever he can grab, and leans between pilots, studying the weather ahead, his voice casual.

WHITE:

Don't look so good, does it? That stuff must go up to thirty thousand feet.

WILLIAMS (to Quincannon):

Think we can get over it?

QUINCANNON (laconic as ever):

Either that or find a hole. Lean 'er back a little. (To White as Williams pulls back mixture controls.) Tell the crew to get on oxygen.

180. INT. DOOR SECTION

McMartin is smoking a cigarette and pointedly ignoring Rader, who lounges beside Weinberg. Things are too tame for Tex, and he watches Tommy out of the corner of his eye as he accepts a light from Weinberg.

TEX:

This airplane reminds me of a Diplodocus.

WEINBERG (blinks):
What's *dat?*

TEX (very seriously):
Prehistoric monster. Had a pinhead but a tail as big as *Mary Ann*'s. In fact, the Diplodocus got so big and cumbersome she couldn't survive. Became extinct a million years ago.

WEINBERG:
How you know what was livin' dat long ago, Lieutenant?

TEX:
Natural history. You oughta read it, Weinberg—it tells all about nature's mistakes. (Weinberg looks skeptical.) Sure, you'll find nature made mistakes just like airplane designers. If you don't believe me, ask the bombardier.

WEINBERG (looks at Tommy):
Dat right, Lieutenant?

McMARTIN (nods sweetly):
Nature made all kinds of mistakes—from the Diplodocus to the louse. (Glances at Tex.) The latter is not extinct.

Weinberg doesn't quite understand the skirmish but before Tex can make a riposte Sergeant White comes barging in with his arms full of oxygen equipment.

WHITE:
Captain says to get on oxygen, sir. We're goin' upstairs. Give me a hand here, Corporal.

181. INT. WAIST SECTION
Winocki, with the dog between his knees, is talking to the kid, who still looks miserable, his head down.

WINOCKI:
You got to be tough, kid. If something gripes you,

keep it here. (Hits his body.) Nobody's gonna soften *me* up. Quincannon would like me to step up and say I was all wrong and hand him a red apple— (Breaks off as White enters with oxygen.)

WHITE:

How'd you like to play nurse, Winocki? (Winocki just looks at him and White hands him oxygen.) I wanta see you put that baby on the bottle. Captain's orders.

Then he ignores Winocki and helps the kid adjust an oxygen tube.

LAP DISSOLVE TO:

182. LONG SHOT OF THE FORTRESS

heading into ugly-looking clouds, climbing more steeply.

LAP DISSOLVE TO:

183. INT. COCKPIT

Not so much light coming through windows now. Thick vapor scudding past. Pilots have oxygen tubes gripped in their teeth and the ship is bouncing around.

WILLIAMS (peering ahead):

See any holes?

QUINCANNON (shakes head):

Pour on more coal.

Williams pulls mixture controls as the ship hits a hard bump.

184. OMITTED

185. INT. WAIST SECTION

Weinberg has joined Winocki and the kid. White is keeping an eye on Chester as he turns on more oxygen. Weinberg watches Winocki, who is holding his hands over the little dog's mouth, feeding him oxygen from a spare bottle. The little dog is strangely trustful and quiet over the uproar of the pulsing, bouncing ship.

WEINBERG (out of the side of his mouth):

He's takin' it like a soldier. Say, dat breath o' life is sure great stuff.

WHITE:

How you feeling, son?

The kid looks up and forces a smile as he nods, though he looks green. White turns on more of the hissing gas.

186. INT. RADIO SECTION

Peterson at radio with oxygen tube gripped in teeth. McMartin and Rader at other side, on oxygen. Ship bouncing. Tommy grins at Tex as he shouts.

McMARTIN:

What's wrong with *Mary Ann?*

Tex holds up his crossed fingers and grins feebly.

187. INT. COCKPIT SHOOTING PAST HEADS OF PILOTS

we see the thick wall of the storm rising to an invisible height. Williams looks at Irish and shakes his head. Irish makes a decision and swings left to parallel the storm front, the ship bumping and groaning. Irish switches on interphone.

QUINCANNON:

Pilot to navigator!

188. INT. MEAT CAN

Hauser catches his sliding instruments as he picks up mikes.

HAUSER:

We can't go off course for more than twenty minutes. Not enough fuel.

189. INT. COCKPIT

QUINCANNON:

Twenty minutes she is. If we don't find a gate, we'll buck through.

WILLIAMS (points):

Irish!

190. SHOOTING PAST THEIR HEADS

we see through the side window what looks like a hole in the dark cloud mass. Irish puts his ship around for it.

191. CLOSE IN TO THEIR FACES

as Quincannon shouts on interphone.

QUINCANNON:

Looks like a break, fellows. Hang on.

192. LONG SHOT OF THE FORTRESS

as she flies into the wall of cloud and vanishes.

193. INT. COCKPIT

Very dark now, the ship bouncing and groaning frighteningly as she hurtles through the dark tunnel.

194. QUICK SHOTS OF THE CREW

in various sections, hanging on, everything bouncing around, no one trying to speak.

195. INT. RADIO SECTION

The ship hits a terrific bump, and the heads of Tex and McMartin almost hit the ceiling, though Peterson hangs onto his desk. As they come down Tex grabs at something and finds it is Tommy's neck. Tommy grins in his face.

McMARTIN:

How you doing, honey?

Tex hurriedly pushes himself off and grabs a brace.

196. LONG SHOT OF THE WALL OF CLOUD
as the fortress suddenly appears out of it and glitters in sudden sunlight.

197. INT. COCKPIT CLOSE ON QUINCANNON AND WILLIAMS
as sunlight floods the compartment and the bumping eases off. Williams heaves a sigh and wipes imaginary sweat off his brow as he looks at Quincannon, who points to the toy elephant.

198. INT. RADIO SECTION
The bumping has eased off rapidly and now Tex and Tommy have collected themselves.

McMARTIN (proud of his airplane):
What d'you think of this B-17 *now?*

TEX:
You mean that little weather we just went through? (Straight-faced.) I knew a fellow in a P-40 once who got caught in a storm over the Atlantic. He wondered why it was so rough till he looked up and saw three ocean liners—he'd flown right through the ocean for ten miles before he realized it—and never hurt his airplane. (Then he grins at Tommy's expression.) Maybe I'm prejudiced.

199. LONG SHOT OF THE FORTRESS
as she pulses on serenely now in fair weather.

FADE OUT

FADE IN

200. INT. CLARK FIELD CONTROL TOWER DAY
The control officer is calling on a hand mike. A radio sergeant sits at the desk which holds the instruments. Behind them a major—Mallory by name and adjutant to the commanding officer—stands looking out a broken window. What we can see of the room has been damaged by explosions. Through the window we glimpse

part of the bomb-pitted field. Smoke drifts across the field, and through it we glimpse tractors working to fill in the holes. In the distance antiaircraft guns pound at intervals and further away is the thudding of big guns.

RADIO (Quincannon's voice):
Zero five five six four to Clark Field—zero five five six four to Clark Field—

CONTROL OFFICER (as Major quickly turns from window):
Clark Field to zero five five six four—go ahead.

QUINCANNON'S VOICE:
Landing instructions for one airplane? How's your field?

CONTROL OFFICER:
Pretty rough, Quincannon. The Japs just had a picnic here and you know how dirty they leave things.

QUINCANNON'S VOICE:
Someday we're going to find a field that's still flat.

CONTROL OFFICER:
Don't come in yet. Keep your altitude till we get number four runway fixed. Tractors working on it now.

QUINCANNON'S VOICE (laconically):
Sorry. Have to come straight in. Almost out of fuel. (Captain reacts and looks at the major questioningly.)

MAJOR MALLORY:
Tell him to come in low over the fence.

CONTROL OFFICER:
Come in low over the fence at the south end. Cut it close to the wire—the north end's shot to pieces.

LAP:

201. EDGE OF FIELD

Shooting slightly up past a barbed-wire fence we see the looming shape of *Mary Ann* heading in through drifting smoke and hear the roar of her engines. She is dropping fast, right at the wire!

202. SHOOTING ALONG FENCE

As she swoops in we see the wheels just clear but the tail wheel catches the top wire, and fence and fence posts fly into the air and go looping after the plane. Camera pans as she rolls to a stop, braked by the wire but undamaged.

LAP:

203. WIDE ANGLE ON MARY ANN

The crew are piling out—unshaven, used up, but undaunted. A tractor comes speeding out from side of field and goes around to tail, ground crew men running after it. Major Mallory jumps off the tractor.

204. NEAR DOOR OF MARY ANN

Mallory strides in as Quincannon jumps down, the other officers taking their turn behind him. Mallory answers Quincannon's salute with a warm handshake.

MALLORY:

Hello, Quincannon—didn't I teach you at Kelly Field how to get over a fence?

QUINCANNON:

That's one way to stop quick, sir. (Then grins sheepishly.) Guess I'm a little tired.

MALLORY:

After seven thousand miles of continuous flying you've got a right to be tired. You've done a great job, all of you— (Sees Rader climb out, with surprise.) Hello, Rader—don't tell me *you've* joined the bombers.

TEX (grins and shakes):

No, sir—I still belong to the opposition.

MALLORY (grins at Quincannon):

I can see you've had a fine time.

QUINCANNON:

Give him a pursuit ship, Major—he still likes to play with toys.

TEX (grins):

It ain't that, Irish. I don't like airplanes—too big. My mother was scared by the Empire State Building. (Ground crew sergeant has stepped in to Mallory.)

SERGEANT:

Wire's clear, sir. No damage.

MALLORY:

Good. Pull her over to the side and get in a full load of gas. (To Quincannon.) Drop out your extra tanks and get her ready for action.

QUINCANNON:

Crew's pretty tired, sir. They really need a rest.

MALLORY (nods sympathetically):

The Japs have been hitting us with sixty bombers at a clip. You've got to be ready to take off before they come back. You're wide open on the ground.

WHITE (who has entered):

Engines are pretty rough, sir. They need an overhaul.

MALLORY:

Do what you can for 'em, Sergeant. But keep 'em running.

WHITE (with eager pride):

Excuse me, sir. I've got a boy stationed here—Lieutenant White. (A hardly discernible reaction in Mallory's eyes.) I'd like to find out about him, sir.

MALLORY:

Have your captain ask the CO when he reports. (To Quincannon.) Colonel Blake wants to see you as soon as your airplane's ready. I'll come back for you. Rader, you can come along with me now.

He turns away abruptly and White looks after him uneasily for just an instant, then snaps out of it.

WHITE:

All right, fellow—let's roll her!

LAP:

205. EDGE OF FIELD FULL SHOT OF MARY ANN
with both ship's crew and ground crew swarming over her.

206. QUICK SHOTS OF BUSINESS OF READYING THE AIRPLANE
The extra gas tanks dropped out of bomb bays. Weinberg working on an engine. Extra ammunition going into guns. White is everywhere, ordering, checking, doing work himself. They have no fuel truck but are pouring in gas from drums and with buckets.

207. NEAR DOOR OF AIRPLANE
White has given swift orders to all the crew except Winocki. Now White comes striding past Winocki, who stands waiting with the dog under his arm.

WHITE:

Get over to the personnel office and see if they'll give you a transfer. We'll need someone to replace you. (Strides on past.) Get rid of that dog, too.

Winocki gives him a defiant look and starts off. Pan on him bringing in Quincannon.

QUINCANNON:

Winocki! (Winocki stops defiantly.) You *want* to get out of this crew?

WINOCKI (not giving an inch):
That's what *you* want, isn't it, sir?

QUINCANNON:
No.

WINOCKI (stares at him):
You mean you'd take all that stuff I've handed you?

QUINCANNON (looks at him for an instant, man to man):
I've been wrong more times than you have.

WINOCKI (the ground cut from under his feet):
I'm beginning to doubt that, sir. I just want to tell you—

QUINCANNON (cuts in, seeing it's all right now):
Turn over that dog to the nearest marine and get back here and check those guns. Give 'em a good goin' over.

WINOCKI:
Yes, sir.

Quincannon watches him with satisfaction as he hurries off with new energy.

208. CLOSE SHOT WEINBERG
working amongst several members of the ground crew. Smoke drifts across them and Weinberg coughs. Turns to the ground crew sergeant.

WEINBERG:
Hey, Sarge—what started all dem fires around duh field?

SERGEANT (grimly):
Fifth column, Corporal. (Weinberg looks at him blankly.) Japs here on the island set brush fires to guide their bombers in.

SECOND SOLDIER:
That ain't all they done, neither. They cut our telephone lines—just before that first sneak attack—

THIRD SOLDIER:
Yeah, while Tokyo was still givin' us love an' kisses on the radio.

SERGEANT:
We didn't have any communication between our airfields—

SECOND SOLDIER:
Our listening posts was cut off too. They couldn't give us no warning.

WEINBERG:
Chee, dat ain't war—dat's moider.

208A. UNDER OPEN BOMB DOORS

Peterson helping a ground crew man roll a big bomb under the plane.

PETERSON:
I sure wish I had an apple.

GROUND CREW MAN (pushing the bomb):
This is the only kind of apples they grow here, buddy.

PETERSON:
Say, I'm gonna write home to send me some apples.

GROUND CREW MAN:
Where's home?

PETERSON:
Minnesota.

GROUND CREW MAN:
You better plant a tree, buddy. Be quicker.

He crawls under bomb bay as they begin hoisting the big bomb up inside the plane.

209–10. OMITTED

211. JUNGLE NEAR FIELD

Winocki is handing the dog, Tripoli, to a sawed-off runt of a marine sergeant named Callahan, who is standing guard beside a wrecked B-17.

WINOCKI:

Don't forget to feed him, Sergeant.

CALLAHAN:

Say, he's gonna eat like a company commander.

WINOCKI (looks at wrecked plane):

What happened to this one?

CALLAHAN:

Air raid! We got seven of 'em spread around the field like this. I'm standin' guard till the demolition squad gets around.

212–13. OMITTED

LAP DISSOLVE TO:

214. INT. CO'S OFFICE (PROCESS)

Quincannon has already reported. He stands with Williams, McMartin, and Hauser facing the CO. Mallory stands nearby. The building which houses this office has been damaged by explosions. The door hangs on its hinges and the window is shattered. Through the openings we can see a scout plane landing through drifting smoke and see Moran coming toward the door. Mallory watching him coming. The CO is looking at the four young officers:

CO:

That's the situation as it stands now. I've given you the blunt facts and given them to you straight—because I know that's the way you want them.

QUINCANNON:

Yes, sir.

CO:

We've taken a shellacking here because we're outnumbered ten to one. Yet every time we've been up against them we've outfought them *five* to one. In other words, if we had one plane to every five of theirs we'd blast 'em off the earth—the record proves it. (Grimly.) From now on our job is to keep fighting with what we've got until the folks back home build us enough airplanes to settle the score.

MALLORY (calls his attention as Moran appears in doorway):

Lieutenant Moran, sir.

CO (turns quickly as Moran salutes):

What did you find, Moran?

MORAN (steps in):

That PT boat was right, sir—it's an invasion fleet. Six transports with landing barges and an escort of destroyers.

CO:

Where?

MORAN:

About forty miles off Lingayen last time I saw 'em, sir. (Grins toughly.) I didn't have much time to hang around. The sky suddenly got full of Zeros—I hiked for home. (Puts chart on desk.) I've marked their position and course on this chart, sir. A flight of B-17s could give 'em a nice party.

CO:

We haven't got any flight of B-17s.

QUINCANNON (eagerly):

You've got one, sir—loading up now.

CO (looks at him keenly for a moment before speaking):

You want to tackle it?

QUINCANNON:

Yes, sir.

Even then the CO hesitates. But finally he picks up the marked chart and extends it to him.

CO:

Study this first. Take your time and don't take any chances. Moran, you go along to their airplane—tell them all you can.

MORAN:

Yes, sir.

They all turn to go, elatedly, then Quincannon stops.

QUINCANNON:

Oh, excuse me, sir. I promised our crew chief I'd ask about his son, Lieutenant White—Danny White.

The CO looks at him queerly and then reaches out to a small pile of personal things and pushes them across the desk toward Quincannon. They all look at:

215. INSERT

A wristwatch, cigarette case, a pair of wings, and a few other trifles.

216. CLOSE GROUP SHOT

Quincannon's eyes are suddenly sick as he looks up at the quiet CO. For a moment no one can speak.

QUINCANNON:

When did it happen, sir?

CO:

Yesterday . . . One of our bombers did a great job—sank a battleship of the Kongo class—they were out of ammunition, coming in for a landing, when the Japs dropped a bomb on the runway, right in front of their B-17. They hit the crater and—well, there wasn't much left. (Gestures toward the few things on his desk.) He was copilot. Fine boy. (Wearily.) I was going to tell Sergeant White myself, but since you're going on this mission . . .

Mallory steps quickly to the door at the sound of a siren suddenly raising its wail at some distance above the sounds of gunfire. Quincannon, his gaze on the trinkets, hardly notices it at first. Then another siren takes it up, nearer. Then one quite close.

CO:

They don't give us much rest, do they? Get to your airplane. Get off the ground before their bombers get over us.

QUINCANNON:

Yes, sir.

He strides out quickly after Moran, the others following. The CO watches them with shadowed eyes, proud of them and yet sorry for them. More sirens screaming now.

217. JUNGLE NEAR FIELD

Four P-40s are hidden under trees and camouflage. Pilots are running to them as mechanics start the engines and hop out. The first pilot guns his engine and taxis out under the heavy trees, then the second, then the third, all following.

218. CLOSE SHOT FOURTH PLANE

Tex Rader, in a flying suit, parachute buckled on, climbs into the cockpit and guns the motor.

219. EDGE OF FIELD MED. LONG SHOT

as the P-40s emerge from undergrowth, engines roaring, one after another.

220. SIDE OF FIELD FULL SHOT MARY ANN

The men are working like beavers as Quincannon and his officers come running in along the side with Lieutenant Moran. The sirens are screaming and we hear the roar of the pursuit ships taking off. Quincannon shouts orders we cannot hear above the din, motioning to this man and that of the crew, as Williams and McMartin climb in the airplane hurriedly. Hauser remains a moment by the door gesticulating over the chart with Moran who is giving final directions. Quincannon makes his way to where Sergeant White is helping load a big shiny thousand-pound bomb from a dolly.

221. BESIDE BOMB SECTION

of the airplane. White is down on his knees as the ground crew men roll the big bomb under the bay. Quincannon taps him on the shoulder. Now the roar of the P-40s is dying away but the sirens still scream, and in the distance we hear antiaircraft begin to pound.

QUINCANNON (shouts in his ear):

How many loaded?

WHITE:

Three! All big ones—thousand pounders!

QUINCANNON:

That's enough. Get those bomb doors closed! Man the ship for takeoff.

WHITE (nods and shouts):

Did you find out about Danny?

At that instant another siren very near begins its hair-raising screech, drowning all chance of talk. Quincannon pulls his hand out of his pocket and thrusts the watch, cigarette case, and pair of wings into White's hands and turns away abruptly. White looks at them for a dazed second and then he shoves them in his pocket and yells to the feverishly working men.[3]

WHITE:

Get 'er out! Roll 'er free!

He motions up into bomb bay and yells something we cannot hear, and the big bomb doors begin closing as the ground crew rolls the fourth bomb back away from the ship. White crawls out and runs for the doorway.

222–24. OMITTED

225. FIELD

Shooting past the backs of Mallory and the CO we see *Mary Ann* go roaring along the runway, her four great engines thundering as she lifts up through the drifting smoke and clears the trees at the far end.

LAP:

226. MARY ANN FROM CAMERA PLANE

The fortress roars along, leveling off now. We are near enough to make out her name on the fuselage.

227. INT. COCKPIT

Quincannon watches straight ahead with a tense face. Williams keeps watching all around but finally broaches the thing that weighs on both their minds.

WILLIAMS:

Did you tell Robbie?

Quincannon nods and Williams stares straight ahead, his face tightening.

228. INT. WAIST SECTION CLOSE TWO-SHOT

Weinberg and Winocki, back to back as they watch out both sides, standing at their guns.

WEINBERG:

Chee, I bet you're wishin' now we had a coupla tail guns.

WINOCKI (growls as he pats his gun):
Don't worry about *Mary Ann.*

WEINBERG (turns around as if he hadn't heard right):
What'd you *say?*

WINOCKI:
What's wrong with these side guns?

WEINBERG (round-eyed):
Say, are you feelin' all right, Joe?

Winocki doesn't answer him, watching grimly for enemy planes.

229. INT. RADIO SECTION

The kid is on radio watch. He stands up, trying to get a look through the window, as Sergeant White pulls his head down out of the top turret.

KID:
See anything, Sergeant?

White shakes his head and pats him on the shoulder encouragingly as he exits along the catwalk, something on his mind.

230. INT. MEAT CAN

Hauser over the marked chart, checking the course. McMartin in the nose, watching down at the sea ahead.

HAUSER:
We're thirty miles off the coast, Tommy. Don't you see anything yet?

McMARTIN:
Nope. Pretty cloudy. (White crawls through the hatch.)

WHITE:
Sight 'em, sir?

HAUSER (worried):
Not yet, Robbie.

McMARTIN:
Wait a minute—

White quickly drops down beside him and both peer out.

231. SHOOTING PAST THEIR HEADS THROUGH PLEXIGLAS NOSE
we see a break in the clouds ahead and below, and through the break a tiny fleet of ships, like toys on a floor of burnished steel. White sings out as they vanish again under cloud.

WHITE:
There they are!

McMARTIN:
Bombardier to pilot! Did you see that flock of ducks down there?

232. INT. COCKPIT
Quincannon and Williams watching down.

QUINCANNON:
Do you think I'm blind? Come on, let's make some duck soup.

McMARTIN'S VOICE:
How would you like chop suey?

QUINCANNON:
Sukiyaki, you flathead. (Noses ship down.) Pilot to crew! Hold your hats, boys— Going down!

233. INT. MEAT CAN CLOSE ON WHITE AND McMARTIN
as the latter gets set in his chair and begins adjusting his bombsight. There is a curious emotion in White's grim face as he touches Tommy's arm.

WHITE:

Will you let me lock up, sir?

McMARTIN:

Sure, Robbie.

White grips a lever beside the bombardier and begins to pull it.

234. INT. BOMB BAY CLOSE SHOT
on the safety pins being pulled out of the three heavy bombs, making them ready for firing.

235. INT. MEAT CAN
White lets go of the lever and nods to McMartin gruffly.

WHITE:

Thanks, sir.

Then swiftly he passes Hauser and crawls through the hatch to get to his station.

236. LONG SHOT MARY ANN FROM CAMERA PLANE
as the fortress noses down through a cloud bank and levels off. Shrapnel puffs begin to burst around her.

237. INT. COCKPIT
Through windows we see shell bursts and hear them above the roar of engines as Quincannon switches on interphone.

QUINCANNON:

Pilot to bombardier. Leveling off. Indicated altitude eighty-six hundred feet.

238. INT. MEAT CAN
McMartin over bombsight making adjustments, his eyes glued to the telescope. Shrapnel bursts are visible through glass nose.

McMARTIN:

Okay. That's eight seven five zero true. Hold it there.

QUINCANNON'S VOICE:

Are you ready for the run?

McMARTIN:

Ready. (Pulls a lever and we hear grind of gears.) Bomb bay doors opening.

239. SHOT UNDER PLANE
showing the big doors yawning open.

240. INT. MEAT CAN

McMARTIN:

Bomb doors open. Check instruments. Speed three two zero.

QUINCANNON'S VOICE:

Check! How do you want it, blindman?

McMARTIN:

Make your run in diagonally. Give me a nice long run and I'll break some clay pigeons for you.

241. INT. COCKPIT

QUINCANNON:

Don't break 'em for *me*—break 'em for Danny White. (Sets AFCD.) Okay. She's all yours.

242. INT. MEAT CAN CLOSE SHOT McMARTIN
He freezes over his bombsight, becomes a part of it now. He pays no attention to the shrapnel bursts ahead.

243. SHOOTING DOWN PAST HIS HUNCHED FIGURE
we can see the fleet of transports and destroyers, their antiaircraft guns flashing in yellow spurts.

244. BOTTOM TURRET FLASH ON PETERSON
as he watches down through his shell, folded like an embryo in a glass womb.

245. TOP TURRET CLOSE ON WHITE'S GRIM FACE
as he stands at his gun, unable to see below but waiting.

246. INT. RADIO SECTION CLOSE SHOT KID
as, earphones clamped to his head, he stands, trying to see down through window.

247. INT. WAIST WEINBERG AND WINOCKI
standing at their guns, paying no attention to the ships below but scanning the sky for fighters. Through windows we see the puffs of breaking shells.

WEINBERG:

> Hey, dem shells is pretty when dey bust— (One bursts very near and we hear its ker-poooom and Weinberg instinctively ducks his head.) Maybe I'm wrong, Joe!

248. INT. MEAT CAN CLOSE SHOT McMARTIN
frozen over his bombsight. He touches the bomb release.

249. NEAR SHOT MARY ANN
as the three big bombs fall from her in a lazy string.

250. SEA LEVEL LONG SHOT ON A CRUISER AND TWO TRANSPORTS
with destroyers racing past to lay heavy smoke screens, guns flashing from all their decks. Then there are three mighty explosions, one a direct hit and two near-misses. (Shots ad lib from miniature stuff.)

251. INT. TOP TURRET CLOSE ON WHITE'S FACE
He grips his gun, waiting tensely as he presses his left

hand against his headphone, his right hand gripping his gun.

QUINCANNON'S VOICE (laconically):
Pilot to bombardier—what happened?

McMARTIN:
Ask Peterson—I can't see.

QUINCANNON'S VOICE:
How about it, Peterson?

PETERSON'S VOICE:
One hit and two near-misses, sir! Looks to me like a cruiser and two transports sinking!

Slowly White reaches into his pocket and pulls out the handful of trinkets Quincannon gave him in such a hurry, and looks at them—the first moment he has been able to relax. Then suddenly something lets go inside of him and for an instant he breaks completely. Savagely he shoves the things back in his pocket and grips his gun with both hands, choking back the thing that is tearing at his insides.[4]

LAP DISSOLVE:

252–53. OMITTED

254. LONG SHOT MARY ANN FROM CAMERA PLANE
As she starts nosing down we see six Zeros come diving out of the cloud bank above, tiny and black against the sky as they go screaming down for *Mary Ann*'s tail.

255. OMITTED

256. TOP TURRET CLOSE SHOT WHITE
as he glances around and then up. Reacts and sings out on interphone.

WHITE:
Fighters!

257. INT. COCKPIT

The pilots react as Irish quickly levels off.

QUINCANNON:

> Take your time, fellows! Sing out if they get on our tail and I'll kick her around. Lead 'em plenty and make it count!

Over this last we hear the machine guns begin to cut loose in the aftersection.

258. MED. LONG SHOT FROM CAMERA PLANE

The bomber's guns are spurting fire as the Japs come roaring down, making successive passes. One of the Zeros is hit and goes smoking down in a spin.

259. OMITTED

260. LONG SHOT FROM HIS ANGLE MARY ANN

as the five remaining Zeros zoom up ahead of her and climb for another attack on her tail.

261. OMITTED

262. LONG SHOT MARY ANN

as she maneuvers, trying to gain altitude. One of the Zeros dives down, making a pass but missing. The bomber's guns are firing.

263. NEARER SHOT FROM CAMERA PLANE

Now we see her top and waist guns blasting as with a screaming roar another Zero comes down on the tail. Quincannon kicks the ship around as much as he can and a slide gun gets the Jap who goes into a spin. Then another Zero comes diving down and the guns blast again.

264–68. OMITTED

269. INT. COCKPIT OF MARY ANN

Williams is looking back through window as Irish kicks ship around again.

WILLIAMS:

Two more on our tail! (Ducks his head as bullets smash through the window.)

269A. INSERT THE TINY TOY AVIATOR

is cut from its string by a bullet and falls to:

269B. FLOOR CLOSE SHOT

as the toy rolls under Quincannon's feet and lies there unnoticed.

269C. CLOSE TWO-SHOT

We hear the guns blasting in the airplane as Quincannon maneuvers, Williams watching out the bullet-punctured window and giving him hand signals.

270. INT. TOP TURRET

Sergeant White cuts loose with his gun.

271. INT. BOTTOM SECTION

Peterson firing at Zero which hurtles under the ship and climbs for another pass.

272. INT. WAIST SECTION

Weinberg fires a burst but then he can swing his gun no further—the enemy is out of range. Winocki sets himself, waiting.

273. SHOOTING ACROSS WINOCKI'S SHOULDER

and gun barrel we see a Zero diving in. He swings the sights on it and waits until it cuts loose. A couple of bullets cut through the window beside his head and then he cuts loose and through the spurting fire of his gun we see the Jap hit and wing over in a smoking spin earthward.

274. CLOSE SHOT INTO WINOCKI'S FACE
as he keeps firing after it.

275. LONG SHOT MARY ANN
She turns again slightly, maneuvering for fighting position. One of the Jap planes comes diving down on the tail.

275A. INT. COCKPIT CLOSE ON IRISH AND WILLIAMS
For a moment the guns have ceased firing. Williams twists around in his seat, trying to see where the attackers are but unable to see the Zero coming down on the tail. The voice of Tex Rader comes sharply over the radio.

TEX'S VOICE:
Rader calling Quincannon! Rader calling Quincannon!

QUINCANNON (throws switch):
Where are you, Tex?

TEX'S VOICE:
We're looking for you, Irish. You forgot your umbrella!

QUINCANNON:
We're five miles north of the field! Coming in at six thousand!

TEX'S VOICE:
I see you! (Then very sharply.) *Hey, look out—they're coming down on your tail!*

The guns begin to pound as Quincannon kicks the ship around. We glimpse the Zero as it screams down past the fortress. In that instant bullets rip through the fuselage and window behind Quincannon and the impact of one in the back throws him across the controls against the instrument panel.

275B. LONG SHOT MARY ANN FROM CAMERA PLANE
She goes into a flat spin as another Zero comes diving down on her tail.[5]

276–79. OMITTED

280. INT. COCKPIT CAMERA ANGLES IN CLOSE BEHIND QUINCANNON
and we see he has been flung forward across the controls and instrument panel, and we also see the bullet hole which is staining the back of his shirt. He pushes himself back into his seat with an effort as Williams, who has been struggling with his controls to get the ship out of the spin in spite of Quincannon's weight against the controls, yells—not realizing Irish was hit.

WILLIAMS (the sky is careening past windows):
Are you all right?

QUINCANNON (gripping controls now):
Yeah—get 'em out—jump! (Williams pulls himself out of his chair with an effort and grips Quincannon's arm, but Irish shakes his head.) *I'll use—escape hatch! Go on—get 'em out!*

280A. LONG SHOT MARY ANN
She is descending crazily in a wide spiral as four P-40s come screaming down out of the clouds above and attack the remaining Zeros which are after the fortress.

281. INT. DOOR SECTION
Sergeant White trips the door and it is flung out of sight by the blast of air. Now we see the sky whirling crazily and hear the scream of the spinning plane. Weinberg and Winocki come jumping into compartment from the waist section. The kid runs in from radio section followed by Peterson. The next instant Hauser and McMartin come tumbling in from forward, followed by Williams. Everyone is hanging on to keep from being thrown from his feet by the spinning plane. White

blocks the open doorway, waiting for an order from the captain, his headphones still on. But Williams yells out to him as he comes tumbling in and motions for them to bail out. White swiftly inspects their parachute harness as he motions them one after another and they jump out into the whirling void—first the kid, then Peterson, then Weinberg, Hauser, and McMartin. He motions Winocki but Winocki seems not to see it as he hangs on to a brace. Williams yells for White to jump, but White nods and pantomimes for Williams to go first—and he does. Then White motions to Winocki, though we cannot hear voices now above the screaming uproar. Winocki steps to the door and then unexpectedly gives White a shove, and White, his back half to the door, pitches out with a surprised expression on his face. Instantly Winocki starts forward, grabbing whatever he can to stay on his feet.

282. INT. COCKPIT

Quincannon has been fighting to hold the controls but suddenly his strength goes and he falls in a faint across the controls again, just as Winocki springs in from the catwalk. Winocki grabs him by the shoulder and pulls him back into the chair, yelling and motioning for him to get out. Then he realizes with an awful look on his face that Irish is unconscious. For an instant Winocki looks at him blankly, and then he pulls him back against the bulkhead so his weight will not be on the controls, and clambers into the copilot's seat and begins to fight the controls. The sky is gyrating crazily and the screaming has intensified to an unbearable pitch. Suddenly the four engines go dead and there is only a whistling sound as Winocki fights the controls blindly and the sky begins to whirl more slowly.

LAP:

283. CLEARING IN JUNGLE NEAR CLARK FIELD

Two soldiers are coming toward camera lugging a machine gun. They suddenly stop short and stare wildly at:

284. REVERSE ACROSS THEM

Through a narrow opening between trees the huge airplane is sailing in straight at camera and settling fast. The soldiers drop flat on their faces and the plane just clears camera.

285. REVERSE SHOOTING ACROSS THE PRONE SOLDIERS

We see the big bomber go miraculously through the clearing between trees and undergrowth and her wheels touch ground and she rolls on bumpily and finally noses over and then falls back on her tire-punctured wheels.[6]

SLOW DISSOLVE TO NIGHT:

286. TENT IN JUNGLE NEAR EDGE OF FIELD (STUDIO)

Just a tent fly with open sides, hedged in by thick jungle growth. The only light is from a lantern hung from the tent pole. In the distance the sky glows from fires. A couple of sentries stand guard outside. The CO sits at a pine table under lantern while Major Mallory stoops over, checking some personnel lists with him. Thudding of big guns continues during whole sequence, punctuated now and then by machine gun bursts as outposts in the jungle, some near some far. Out of the darkness comes the ground crew sergeant we already know. The sentry stops him, then lets him pass as he recognizes him. Camera moves in on CO as the sergeant enters the lantern light under the tent-fly and salutes. Mallory straightens up.

MALLORY:

Well, Sergeant?

SERGEANT:

If we had ten days and plenty of spare parts I'd say we might get her to fly again, sir.

CO:

I don't know if we have twenty-four hours. The enemy's landing a lot of troops.

SERGEANT:

I counted over two hundred bullet holes in her, sir. Props all bent. Controls in a mess. Wheels damaged, tires flat, one fuel tank punctured, tail shot to pieces. She's a washout—I don't see how they brought her down in one piece.

CO:

Neither do I. (To Mallory.) Looks like we'll have to write off *Mary Ann*, Major. Our last B-17.

MALLORY (nods):

Nothing else to do except destroy her. (Turns to sergeant.) I'll send a demolition squad in the morning. No use making any more fires tonight—they'd only hit us again.

SERGEANT:

Yes, sir. (Exits.)

CO (to Mallory):

Where's the remainder of her crew?

MALLORY:

Hospital, sir. Quincannon wanted to see them.

CO:

How is he? (Mallory shakes his head.)

LAP:

287. INT. HOSPITAL (STUDIO)

White and the rest grouped closely around Quincannon, who lies on an army cot in corner of wrecked frame building. Roof blown off, only few boards left, and through opening we hear dull thudding of big guns and staccato bursts of machine guns. Doctor stooped over Irish giving him a shot of adrenalin (this business in group shot so we don't see it too clearly). Utter silence in room and nobody moves. Camera moves in slowly past standing men close on Quincannon and doctor, who has now put his hypodermic aside and is stooped over

Quincannon watching him closely for reaction. Camera moves in to close-up as Quincannon's eyes open and he looks foggily past camera at:

288. REVERSE ON SILENT GROUP OF STANDING MEN
strained, silent, watching. (Through whole scene it is reaction on men of Quincannon's dying that is our dramatic and emotional material.)

QUINCANNON'S VOICE (weakly):
Hello, chief.

WHITE:
Hello, skipper.

He steps forward, something in his hand. The others don't move.

289. CLOSE ANGLE ON COT
as White steps in to Quincannon, shooting past doctor, who has straightened up and stepped back a little.

QUINCANNON (weak, trying to account for everyone, but seeing foggily):
Everyone okay?

WHITE (gruffly):
Yes, sir. (Shows the toy mascot in his hand.) Got a chip in him, but he's still okay, too.

QUINCANNON:
Thanks.

He tries to lift his arm from the coverlet but can't make it. White puts the toy in his hand and his fingers grip it tightly, the hand lying on the coverlet. White steps back out of frame as Quincannon keeps trying to see all the faces.

QUINCANNON:
Where's that pursuit pilot? . . . Tex?

290. GROUP SHOT
as Tex straightens up, holding his rifle.

TEX:
Here, Irish.

QUINCANNON (sees him more clearly):
What you doing with that rifle?

WEINBERG:
He's infantry now, skipper. Dey took his airplane away from him. He was usin' up Japs so fast dey was afraid dey wouldn't be none left to surrender.

291. VERY CLOSE SHOT QUINCANNON'S FACE
and we see an anxiety come into it.

TEX:
That's right, skipper—some of it. No more airplanes.

Quincannon's eyes go wide with anxiety. This is his first doubt that the *Mary Ann* is okay.

QUINCANNON:
Winocki.

WINOCKI:
Yes, sir?

292. CLOSE ON WINOCKI AND WHITE
standing stiffly, afraid now of what Irish is going to ask.

QUINCANNON:
They told me you brought *Mary Ann* in.

WHITE (as Winocki doesn't answer):
He did, sir.

292A. GROUP SHOT
as Quincannon stares at Winocki, trying to hold on him.

WINOCKI:

She came in herself. I just sat there. She knew you were still in the office.

WEINBERG (eagerly):

Sure she did. She knowed all duh time de skipper was settin' dere watchin' her. She had to act like a lady.

QUINCANNON (staring at Winocki queerly):

Thanks. (With effort.) She all right? (Winocki doesn't answer.) She is all right, isn't she? (Winocki doesn't answer.)

292B. CLOSE SHOT WHITE

his face contorted with repressed anguish.

QUINCANNON (imperatively, as White is silent):

Tell me, Robbie. What's wrong with her?

WHITE:

Props. Gear. One wing tip. That's all.

292C. GROUP SHOT

Quincannon very feeble but agitated, his eyes wide now.

QUINCANNON:

That's all. Just a wing gone. Gone.

WHITE (in protest):

No, I tell you. Just a tip. What's a wing tip? Just a couple of days.

QUINCANNON (blurrily):

Two days?

WHITE:

Yes, sir. *Sure.* (Looks around at the others; then, emphatically.) Two days!

QUINCANNON (feebly; with a kind of panic):
Wait a minute . . . don't go . . . don't go . . . wait for me, fellows. . . .

His fingers relax and the toy rattles to the floor as his whole excited body relaxes and his eyes close. The doctor steps in quickly and stoops over him, masking his face from camera. None of the men moves but there is an agony of questioning in their faces as they watch the doctor.

WHITE (choking):
Doctor!

The doctor straightens up, still masking Quincannon's face from camera, and lays Quincannon's limp arms across his chest without replying to White. The big guns go on thudding as we

FADE OUT

FADE IN DAY

293. CO'S TENT IN JUNGLE EDGE OF FIELD (STUDIO)
It is next morning and the CO, in shirt-sleeves and looking as worn as the rest of the officers and men we have seen, is seated on a campstool signing some evacuation orders which Mallory is placing before him on the pine table. The thudding of the big guns seems to have come nearer over the fade, and now and then there are machine gun bursts off in the jungle. Through the open wall of the tent fly we see two soldiers helping a wounded man between them, passing on through the clearing. The demolition squad enters and their corporal goes toward:

294. NEAR SHOT CO AND MALLORY
They look up as the unkempt, unshaven, tough-looking corporal enters carrying a queer assortment of gear—sticks of dynamite, coils of wire, an exploder, and so on.

MALLORY:
Yes, Corporal?

CORPORAL (aggrievedly):
Dey's something wrong, sir. Me and duh squad think dey's something wrong. (Indicates off.)

295. CLOSE GROUP SHOT OF FIVE DISHEVELED-LOOKING SOLDIERS
All look equally unshaven and equally tough. Their accoutrements are meant to be a mystery to us for a moment: Two of them carry five-gallon gasoline tins, another has a sledgehammer, another an axe, and the fifth—at the opposite side from the two with the gasoline cans—holds in hand a smoking torch.

296. MED. SHOT ON THE CORPORAL
facing the CO and Mallory. The corporal looks at Mallory and the CO apologetically.

CORPORAL:
We was detailed to boin all dem busted airplanes.

MALLORY (impatiently):
What's wrong?

CORPORAL (uneasily):
Duh Japs is stealin' em, sir.

MALLORY (blows up):
Don't talk nonsense, man! A few Japs have been filtering through our lines but they're only snipers! They're not stealing airplanes!

CO:
Wait a moment, Mallory. (Looks at the corporal, and by now the audience is way ahead of us, as it should be.) You had the wreckage of five B-17s to demolish. Were any of them missing?

CORPORAL (relieved to find someone talking sense to his own plain sense):
Parts of dem—*sure*—I mean, yes, sir.

MALLORY (cuts in impatiently):
Impossible!

CO:

Wait, Mallory— (To the corporal who by this time has no use for Mallory.) There's a wrecked B-17 in the clearing back of this tent. Have you burned it yet?

CORPORAL:

No, sir. We was on our way but I told duh boys we oughta report what dem Japs is doing.

CO (gets up, already half suspecting the truth):

Well, let's go see what they're doing back here. Come on, Major.

LAP DISSOLVE:

297. EDGE OF CLEARING NEAR FIELD SHOOTING TOWARD
some thick jungle vegetation as the CO and Mallory come through, followed by the corporal and his demolition squad. They have to come around a thick clump before they can see into the clearing behind camera. Then suddenly they stop short near camera and their reactions are interesting as they see:

298. REVERSE ANGLE MED. LONG SHOT MARY ANN
in the midst of beehive activity. She is partly dismantled and spare parts from other airplanes are strewn around on the ground. They have rigged a block and tackle from a couple of trees. The bent props have been pulled off and new ones swung on. Sergeant White is on a ladder working at the nearest engine, Hauser helping him. Williams has rescued a lathe from the wrecked machine shop and is driving it by a belt looped over the wheel of a jacked-up truck. Winocki is cutting off a short section of the tail. Weinberg alone is not visible, being inside the plane.

299. REVERSE CLOSE INTO FACES OF THE DISCOVERERS
For an instant the corporal is just as mad as if he had found thieving Japs. He raises an angry arm and points.

CORPORAL:

Dat's duh stuff! Dey swiped it!

Pushes forward past the officers indignantly.

300. WIDE ANGLE ON MARY ANN

and the busy crew as the corporal and his squad march in. The corporal gives the ladder on which White is working an angry shake.

CORPORAL:

Git down, Sergeant!

WHITE (grabs engine to steady himself and growls down):

Get away, you!

CORPORAL:

I said git down! We're gonna boin dis junk!

WHITE:

You're going to *what?*

CORPORAL:

Boin dis junk! Come on, boys—give her duh torch!

In two bounds White is down the ladder and grabs the torchbearer wrathfully as the rest of the crew comes running.

301. NEAR GROUP SHOT

as the crew confronts the demolition squad. White shoves back the squad leader.

WHITE:

Get that gasoline away from this airplane, you firebugs!

WINOCKI:

And that dynamite, too!

WILLIAMS:

Who gave you orders to destroy government property?

CORPORAL:

Duh CO—dat's who.

WILLIAMS:

Tell the CO to go take a— (Stops as he sees out of corner of his eye the CO coming with Mallory and Moran.) to go take a look at this airplane. (Turns and salutes.) Excuse me, sir—we worked all night on her. She's going to be as good as new.

WHITE:

Better, sir. We got an idea how to put a tail gun in 'er!

302. DOOR OF MARY ANN

Weinberg, who has been working inside, emerges, his face covered with grease. As he leans out and looks off at group we hear

VOICE OF DEMOLITION CORPORAL:

Duh colonel says boin her and she's gonna boin!

303. GROUP IN FRONT OF PLANE

Sergeant White glares at the corporal as Williams turns pleadingly to the CO.

WILLIAMS:

Give us a dozen more men, sir, and we'll have her in the air in twenty-four hours.

CO:

In twenty-four hours this field will be in possession of the enemy. General MacArthur has given the order to withdraw.

They stand in crushed silence as Weinberg pushes in. The demolition corporal opens his eyes wide.

CORPORAL:

Weinberg!

WEINBERG (stares):
Chee, Butch, I t'ought you was still on dat streetcar in Joisey.

CORPORAL:
I wisht I was, Weinberg, I wisht I was. I never enlisted to be no fireman.

WHITE (sternly to Weinberg):
If you know that firebug, take him over on that cactus and set down. And shut up when the colonel's speaking.

CO:
I appreciate what you've tried to do—but our job now is to destroy everything that can be of use to the enemy. (To McMartin.) Is your bombsight still in this airplane?

McMARTIN:
Yes, sir.

WILLIAMS:
We won't let it be taken, sir.

HAUSER:
Nor *Mary Ann* either! We'll get her out of here.

WHITE (with emotion):
We'll burn her ourselves if we can't make it.

WILLIAMS (begging):
That's right, sir—I give you my word.

CO (looks at them a moment):
Very well, Williams—I'll take your word.

WHITE (from his heart):
Thank you, sir.

CO:
I hope you all know what you're doing. You'll soon be alone at this field. You know what will happen if

the Jap moves in here while you're still on the ground?

WILLIAMS:
I think we do, sir.

CO (turns to demolition corporal):
Leave materials here for destroying this airplane.

CORPORAL:
Yes, sir.

Lieutenant Moran enters and salutes the CO.

MORAN:
Excuse me, sir—but they've got that scout plane patched up. I'm ready to go on reconnaissance, but I can't find my gunner—Sergeant Michaels.

MALLORY (explains to CO):
He volunteered for infantry duty last night—after they cracked up. Probably out in some foxhole.

The CO mulls this for an instant and then turns to Williams.

CO:
I know you're shorthanded but we've got to find out where the enemy's advancing and how far. Which gunner can you spare most easily—for a couple of hours?

KID (steps forward):
Me, sir!

WINOCKI:
Wait a minute, Chester—

KID:
No, Joe— (To CO.) They're all more useful here, sir, than I am.

CO (nods):
Go with Lieutenant Moran.

KID:

Yes, sir.

304. JUNGLE NEAR FIELD WIDE ANGLE ON

the wrecked B-17 we saw in scene 211. The marine sergeant guarding the wreckage, Callahan, is stooped down feeding the little dog out of his mess kit. Out of the edge of jungle steps Tex Rader with a rifle over his shoulder, his face smudged, uniform torn, not the snappy figure we first knew. (Guns thudding and bursts of machine gun off.)

305. MED. SHOT ON CALLAHAN

feeding the dog as Tex limps in on aching feet and looks at the dog.

TEX:

Where'd you find that little beast, Sergeant?

CALLAHAN (proudly):

He's a Marine Corps, dog, Lieutenant.

TEX:

Yeah, I know. (Leans over and snaps his fingers warily.) Hiya, Moto. (Dog snarls.) Cut it out, Moto, I'm your friend. Nice Moto . . . *Moto!* (Dog lunges fiercely and he backs off.) Call him off, Sergeant—I've had enough trouble with Jap snipers without getting hydrophobia.

CALLAHAN:

His name ain't Moto—it's Tripoli.

TEX:

What?

CALLAHAN:

Tripoli! I thought you knowed his trick.

TEX (reaches down cautiously):

Tripoli? (Dog wags his tail and licks Tex's hand.)

CALLAHAN:
Cute trick, ain't it?

TEX (darkly):
Very cute, Sergeant.

Past them we see the demolition squad hurrying into the clearing from field followed by Major Mallory and the CO. The demolition squad goes straight to the plane and begins throwing on gasoline and igniting it.

306. ANOTHER ANGLE
as Mallory and the CO swiftly enter to Tex and Callahan, who salute.

CO:
How's it going out there, Rader?

TEX:
All I got was a foxhole view, sir—with my face in six inches of dirt. They're withdrawing to Bataan. (CO nods gravely.) As I'm not in the regular infantry I thought I'd better report back to the field.

CO (grimly):
Not much left of it. We're getting out too.

MALLORY:
We're moving pilots and ground crews over to Mindanao. May be a chance to get you to Batavia or Port Darwin. They've got plenty of airplanes there.

TEX (indicates burning wreckage):
Is that all you've got left here, sir?

MALLORY:
Except for one patched up scout plane and a B-17 that won't fly.

CO:
The same bomber that ferried you here from Hickam. I know I'm wrong to let 'em work on *that* one.

TEX (reacts):

They're trying to fix up *Mary Ann*, sir?

CO (nods grimly):

I hadn't the heart to refuse 'em. Especially that old sergeant.

MALLORY:

They must have spent all night robbing these other wrecks for spare parts.

307. CLOSE-UP TEX

An inexplicable desire is welling up in him.

308. CLOSE GROUP SHOT TEX, CALLAHAN, MALLORY, AND THE CO

The wreck burns fiercely in background now.

TEX:

Would you let me help 'em, sir?

CO (blows up):

What kind of lunatics have we got in the Air Corps, Mallory? Don't any of 'em know what's impossible?

CALLAHAN (eagerly):

Can't I give 'em a hand, too, sir? (That really floors the two officers.) I don't know nothin' about an airplane but I can do what I'm told.

Tex grins at the speechless CO as we

LAP DISSOLVE:

309. FIELD CLOSE ON PATCHED-UP SCOUT PLANE

Moran is already in the front cockpit as the kid, Chester, climbs in behind him, buckling on his parachute. Engine idling. Moran looks behind questioningly and the kid grins and nods and pats his machine gun as he settles himself behind it. Then Moran opens the throttle and camera pans as the plane scuds down between bomb craters.

310. CLEARING NEAR EDGE OF FIELD FULL SHOT MARY ANN

The crew is fitting a new propellor to number one engine. Williams and White are superintending the job as the others swing the heavy prop from the block and tackle improvised between a couple of trees. We hear the scout plane taking off, and its engine grows louder as it circles toward *Mary Ann*. Tex Rader, Sergeant Callahan, and the little dog come through brush at edge of clearing, making toward the busy group at airplane.

311. CLOSE GROUP SHOT

They squint up as the scout plane roars overhead, climbing, and its shadow flits across them.

WEINBERG:

Dat's duh kid!

WHITE (squinting up):

I don't like him leavin' *Mary Ann* this way. Ain't good luck.

WILLIAMS:

He'll be back in a couple of hours. Come on, don't waste time.

WHITE (snaps out of it):

That's right. You hear what the lieutenant says? Put a little muscle in it now. Get her on the hub. Break your backs!

He grunts with the effort as they all shove on the heavy prop. The sound of the scout plane swiftly fades. There is a bark behind them and they look around to see:

312. TEX RADER, SERGEANT CALLAHAN

and the little dog.

TEX:

Hello, fellows—need any help?

313. ANOTHER ANGLE GROUP SHOT

The reactions on the sweating faces are unusual.

WEINBERG:

Chee, it's duh pursuit pilot. We t'ought you was in duh infantry, Lieutenant.

TEX:

Too hard on the feet. My mother didn't raise me to be a foot soldier.

WILLIAMS:

She raised you to be a pain in the neck.

TEX:

Now is that a way to talk, Bill? I've slogged miles through this jungle just to give you a hand.

McMARTIN:

We're doing all right, Texas.

TEX:

Looks like you boys have picked yourself a job. Can't you use me and the Marine Corps here?

WHITE (to Williams under his breath):

We sure could, sir.

WILLIAMS (stares at Tex):

You're really asking to join our crew?

TEX (grins):

Don't get any false ideas. I'd rather fly than walk—even in that crate. I haven't changed my mind, but I'm willing to work my way.

WHITE (to Williams; aside):

Take him, sir.

WILLIAMS:

All right, Rader, but don't get any false ideas yourself. I wouldn't let you set foot in this airplane again, except we need you.

McMARTIN:

How you getting along with Moto there?

TEX:

I'm getting along fine, Tommy—*with Tripoli*. (As Tommy grins.) I knew it all along, you morons.

McMARTIN:

Listen to him!

TEX (to Williams):

Stop grinning like an ape, headman, and tell me what to do.

WILLIAMS:

We've got to get fuel before they burn the storage tank. Scare up a truck and bring it in drums. Fuel trucks got wrecked.

TEX:

Yes, *sir*.

WILLIAMS:

Take the Marine Corps with you—so you can find your way back. (There is a heavy fusillade of machine gun fire off in the jungle and they all look off.)

WHITE (blasts at them):

Come on, soldiers, that's no layoff whistle! Get to work!

They all double to their task as Tex and Callahan exit.

LAP DISSOLVE TO:

313A. CLEARING NEAR FIELD FULL SHOT MARY ANN

A couple of hours have elapsed and they have made some progress in getting the ship together. Three new props have been fitted on. Now, under the direction of White, they are getting a prop on number one engine. They have rigged a derrick with several cut saplings and are hoisting the heavy prop with a block and tackle. White, McMartin, and Hauser are trying to ease it onto the hub as other members of the crew put their weight on the rope below them. Tex and Callahan are driving a battered truck, which is loaded with gasoline drums, in from the clearing and alongside the plane.

313B. NEAR SHOT GROUP
as they work to get the prop in place. White, perched on the engine, bawls orders hoarsely.

WHITE:
Heave a little. Heave. Hold 'er now. Steady. Steady. (They grunt as they slide the prop into place.) That's got 'er. (Heaves a breath and looks down at them sweatily.) Where's Weinberg?

WILLIAMS (on ground):
He went over to the storeroom, chief, to scare up another can of oil. He'll be back in a minute.

WHITE (puffing with exertion):
Okay, sir. I guess he can handle this now. I got to work on number three engine. (Looks down at the crew who have been heaving on the line.) You fellows can— (Breaks off and looks up.)

Now they all look off where White is looking and we hear the faint sound of:

313C. VERY LONG SHOT
an approaching airplane.

313D. GROUP SHOT
They all squint off as the sound grows plainer. Tex and Callahan duck under the wing and join the group.

WILLIAMS:
Looks like one of ours, Robbie.

WHITE (squinting off):
Yes, sir. Scout plane. Must be the kid comin' back.

But suddenly there is an ugly multimotored drone growing swiftly audible above the thin sound of the incoming scout plane, and they all turn their heads and peer up in the opposite direction.

313E. LONG SHOT
half a dozen Jap planes diving out of a cloud toward the field.

313F. GROUP SHOT
for reactions. All electrified.

McMARTIN (sings out):
Hey, those are Japs!

WHITE:
Zeros and a coupla dive bombers!

WINOCKI:
They're gonna buzz the field!

McMARTIN:
They're gonna blast his airplane!

HAUSER:
She's wide open, Bill! They'll chop her to pieces!

WILLIAMS:
Jump down here! (As they pile down.) Winocki. Peterson. Get those machine guns set up on the ground. Get inside, chief. Take the top turret. Tex. Get on the waist guns. Take the Marine Corps with you. Come on, the rest of you. (Runs around in the direction Winocki and Peterson have gone, the rest following as the angry drone grows swiftly louder.)

313G. FIELD MED. LONG SHOT WEINBERG
as he hurries across the field lugging a heavy five-gallon tin of oil. The drone of the incoming Japs grows louder and we see him try to break into a run, but still hanging on to this load. Then we see a Zero dive low and come skimming along the ground toward him as he runs.

313H. NEAR SHOT WEINBERG
as he runs into camera. We hear the savage roar of the plane and then its machine guns open up. Weinberg stops short and the bullets kick up dirt past his toes. The tin is hit and oil spurts from it. Weinberg looks after the plane triumphantly and makes a contemptuous gesture. Then he sees the oil spurting, grabs up the tin in both arms so that the hole is uppermost, and goes on as fast as he can toward the other side of the field.

313I. FULL SHOT MARY ANN
We see one of the Zeros come zooming at the plane as if it were going to hit it. Opens up with machine guns. Williams and the others blast away with machine guns set up on the ground, and the top turret gun is pounding as the Zero whooshes low over *Mary Ann*. No damage done.

313J. DIVE BOMBER
coming down toward the clearing. They open up with machine guns from the ground around plane. We hear the whistle of the falling bomb but it explodes off in the jungle a hundred yards away, throwing up a great fountain of dirt. The plane roars overhead. Weinberg comes running into the clearing, still hugging his tin of oil. As he comes in another bomb falls a couple of hundred feet away and he drops flat on his belly.

313K. SHOTS AD LIB OF THE STRAFING CLOSE SHOTS OF THE MEN FIRING MACHINE GUNS INTERCUT WITH SHOTS OF THE PLANES WHOOSHING OVERHEAD

313L. LOW CAMERA ON WILLIAMS
He is trying to train a machine gun on another Zero we can hear diving in to strafe the plane. Weinberg crawls in swiftly and tries to help him. But the gun is mounted too low on its tripod to get it up on the plane. Weinberg grabs the barrel and points it up toward the plane as it crescendoes into scene and Williams cuts loose.

313M. LONG SHOT OF THE ZERO
as it fails to lift out of its dive and goes crashing into trees, goes end over end, and burns.

313N. CLOSE ON WILLIAMS AND WEINBERG
Weinberg drops the hot gun barrel and his hands are smoking. But Weinberg, looking up, seems not to notice it as he points up.

WEINBERG:

Look—dey're after duh kid!

Williams looks up at:

313O. SKY SHOT
Dogfight between the scout plane and two Zeros. Moran maneuvers cleverly but his plane is so slow that the odds are hopeless. The Zeros fly rings around him.

313P. GROUP SHOT NEAR MARY ANN
White, Tex, and Callahan have joined the others standing by their guns, helpless to do anything.

314–46. OMITTED (INCLUDED IN ABOVE)

347. SKY SHOT
The scout plane slips off cleverly as one of the Zeros comes down and shoots past it. Then the other Zero starts its dive.

348. CLOSE SHOT MORAN AND CHESTER IN COCKPIT OF SCOUT PLANE PROCESS
The kid is firing down at the plane which has whipped past. Moran looks back over his shoulder and tries to shout a warning as he points up and back, but at that instant we hear the burst of machine guns out of scene and Moran slumps over his controls. The kid tries to get his gun around and up, but the plane heads down in a spin as machine gun bullets riddle the front part of

cockpit. The kid gets the cowling back, pulls himself up with an effort, and jumps out, grabbing for his parachute ring as he vanishes.

349. FLASH OF FACES OF WHITE, McMARTIN, WILLIAMS, HAUSER, AND CREW
watching up.

350–51. OMITTED

352. SKY SHOT
A plummeting body and then suddenly a white flowering of silk and the chute billows out and begins to descend smoothly.

353. CLOSE ON WEINBERG, WINOCKI, PETERSON, AND CREW
for reactions. Weinberg yells out joyously:

WEINBERG:
Dat's doin' it, kiddo!

They are all grinning suddenly with relief. Then suddenly their expressions change and White yells out involuntarily.

WHITE:
Look out! Look out, kid!

354. INCLUDED IN 353

355. WHAT THEY SEE SKY SHOT
A Zero plane is diving toward the billowing parachute, which is now near the field.

356. CLOSE SHOT KID (PROCESS)
floating in his shroud lines. His hair blows in the breeze. Clouds move up in distance behind him, showing his easy swinging descent. Then he swings around and he looks surprised past camera.

357. WHAT HE SEES A JAP ZERO
coming straight toward him. Suddenly its machine gun cuts loose.

358. CLOSE SHOT SWINGING KID
as he looks surprised, incredulous. A couple of shroud lines are cut by the streams of bullets and he grabs at them as if he were only afraid of falling. Instinctively he puts his hand in front of his face as if to ward off the bullets. Then he is hit and his body spins around limply.

359. CLOSE ON FACES OF WHITE AND CREW
for reactions. White draws in his breath sharply through his teeth as if he had taken the bullets in his own body. Weinberg makes a sound of horrified protest in his throat as Winocki, with a look of fury, grabs the machine gun from his shoulder and barges out on the field. Peterson grabs at him and misses as he yells:

PETERSON:
Joe—they'll get you, too!

360–61. INCLUDED IN 359

362. SHOOTING PAST THEM
we see Winocki running out on the pitted field toward where the parachute is settling with its limp burden.

363. LONG SHOT FIELD
As the limp body hits the earth the parachute spills over in the wind and starts dragging the dead kid. The roar of the diving Zeros is ear-splitting as one comes low toward the dragging parachute. From one side we see Winocki running toward the chute recklessly, lugging his gun.

364. SHOT OF THE DEAD KID
being dragged along by the half-spilled chute. The on-

coming plane opens up with its guns, and we see the bullets kicking dust toward the kid, through him, and then on past as the airplane roars over the field. The next instant Winocki reaches it and grabs the half-spilled chute, stopping it. Looks up past camera as we hear the roar of another Zero zooming in. Winocki swings his machine gun around and cuts loose past camera.

365. LONG SHOT FIELD
The low-flying Zero hits the ground and goes end over end with a terrible crashing noise.

366. CLOSE ON WINOCKI
as he whirls around into camera, still gripping his gun.

367. WHAT HE SEES THE ZERO
stopped at far end of field in a mass of wreckage as it bursts into flames.

368. CLOSE INTO WINOCKI'S FACE
He looks at the burning wreckage as if he can hardly believe he brought it down. Then slowly he looks down at the dead kid (out of frame on the ground at his feet) as we

FADE OUT

FADE IN

369. CLEARING NEAR FIELD FULL SHOT MARY ANN NIGHT
(Over the fade the thudding of the big guns has grown much louder and more ominous. Machine gun bursts very near now. Create with sound the feeling of the enemy closing in.) It is near daybreak and the men have toiled all night. The plane once more looks like a ship that might fly. They are working on the engines now. Tex and Callahan are up on one wing pouring gasoline into a fuel vent from buckets.

370. MED. SHOT WHITE
working on an engine. Williams enters to the foot of his ladder, ducking under a wing.

WILLIAMS:
How's she coming, chief?

WHITE:
She's gettin' spark, she's gettin' air, she's gettin' gas. She oughta start next time. What time is it, sir?

WILLIAMS (peers at wristwatch):
Near five A.M.

WHITE:
Soon be daybreak.

WILLIAMS:
Yeah.

White comes down ladder with something on his mind.

371. CLOSE ON WILLIAMS
as White steps down beside him and drops his voice as he motions off where machine gun bursts are close now in the jungle.

WHITE:
Sounds like they're gettin' close, sir.

WILLIAMS (as if he hardly cared):
Yeah.

WHITE (very low):
If we don't get off before daylight— (Hesitates significantly.)

WILLIAMS (in a flat voice):
I'll get everything ready to burn her. (Turns away.)

372. TAIL OF MARY ANN CLOSE ON WINOCKI AND McMARTIN
working. They have cut off a section of tail, and now

Winocki shoves a machine gun into the opening as Williams enters on inspection and looks at it.

WINOCKI:
There she is, sir. The Japs are gonna get a surprise if they come in on the tail of *this* B-17.

WILLIAMS:
Think you can work that gun?

WINOCKI:
Just got room, sir. I tried it.

WILLIAMS:
What about that tail wheel, Tommy?

McMARTIN:
Have to leave it down.

WILLIAMS (nods after a swift inspection):
Okay. Did you get a full bomb load?

McMARTIN (nods):
Full to the gills. I don't know what we're gonna do with 'em but we got 'em.

WILLIAMS:
We can always drop 'em out. (Very near machine gun burst.) You fellows better help Rader with those buckets of gas. Get ready to slop it under the plane.

McMARTIN:
For *what?*

WILLIAMS (grimly):
You know what.

Two of the engines cough and all listen tensely, then as they catch and start to rev up they breathe deeply. Williams hurries out.

373. FRONT OF PLANE

Two of the engines are turning. White and Weinberg look up at them, listening critically. Then White motions up toward cockpit window, and Hauser cuts them down to idling speed as Williams hurries in to White.

WHITE (triumphantly):
That's two of 'em, sir!

WILLIAMS:
We'll need all four to get off.

WHITE:
Weinberg says he's got number three about ready. (Very loud burst of machine gun near in jungle and they glance off.)

WILLIAMS:
That sounds like Peterson. Step on it, Robbie!

374. UNDER FUSELAGE

Tex and Callahan are setting open pails of gasoline under the body of the ship. Winocki and McMartin enter, carrying more pails.

TEX:
Two engines working and you can't get off. A P-40 flies on one. (A third engine coughs and starts.)

McMARTIN (elatedly):
There's number three!

Peterson, who has been standing guard, comes running in.

PETERSON:
Where's Lieutenant Williams?

WILLIAMS (enters from opposite side):
Here, Peterson.

PETERSON (tensely as he indicates toward tail):
Some Japs coming through from that direction, sir. I emptied my machine gun but it won't stop 'em long.

WILLIAMS (swiftly to them all):
Get your guns set up back there. Try and hold 'em off if they come through. Callahan, you stand by these buckets. You too, Tommy. If number four won't start we'll have to burn her. (Growls.) Not you, Tex. If *Mary Ann*'s got to go, we'll do it without any pursuit pilot. Get back there on a gun . . . *Winocki!*

WINOCKI (crowding in):
Yes, sir?

WILLIAMS:
Get inside in that tail. We'll find out if you can work that gun.

WINOCKI:
Yes, sir. (Exits.)

375. MED. SHOT NUMBER FOUR ENGINE
White and Weinberg working on her. The other three engines are idling. They work with desperation checking ignition cables. Williams comes striding under wing and looks up at them tensely.

WILLIAMS:
Japs are coming through, chief!

WHITE (desperately):
Think you can make it with three engines, sir?

WILLIAMS:
On those runways out there? We ought to have five!

WEINBERG (frantically):
I don't get it. She oughta start! Dis ignition's okay!

There is a loud fusillade of shots from the darkness of the jungle and Williams ducks under wing and runs aft.

376. BEHIND TAIL OF SHIP
Peterson and Tex duck their heads as bullets whack into the tail above their heads. Then they begin firing back.

377. UNDER FUSELAGE
McMartin and Callahan standing by the buckets of gasoline as Williams runs in to them. He kicks over buckets of gasoline on the ground under the ship as he comes. Motions to the two waiting men as the shooting grows louder and they dash the contents of their buckets on the underside of plane. Williams motions and yells at them to get back.

378. CLOSE INTO FACES OF WILLIAMS, McMARTIN, AND CALLAHAN
as they back off a safe distance. Williams jerks out a box of matches as he yells into Tommy's ear.

WILLIAMS:

Get Monk and Winocki out! Hurry!

Tommy nods, but just as he starts we hear number four engine cough and then roar into life and Tommy stops. He and Williams look at each other for a frozen moment, fearing the engine will stop. But she grows stronger. Williams waves his arms and lets out a war whoop.

WILLIAMS:

Inside, everybody! Man the ship for takeoff!

379. EXT. DOOR OF MARY ANN WIDE ANGLE
Hauser in doorway, offering a hand, as the men pile into scene from all directions. Callahan is in scene first and Hauser drags him into the plane. Weinberg and White, their faces jubilant, come running in from forward, White still holding a spanner in one greasy hand. McMartin and Williams dash in, all crowding at the

door, Callahan and Hauser now helping drag them into the plane.

380. EDGE OF CLEARING BEHIND THE PLANE
A squad of about a dozen Jap soldiers comes crashing through into view, heading toward plane.

381. CLOSE SHOT ON THE SAWED-OFF TAIL
Winocki, inside the tail, cuts loose with his machine gun, which spurts flame past camera.

382. REVERSE ON THE SQUAD OF JAPS
running toward plane. They are dimly seen but they tumble like tenpins as Winocki's machine gun keeps pounding. One Jap keeps on his feet and comes running on toward camera with his bayoneted rifle.

383. EXT. DOOR OF PLANE
They are all in now except White and Williams. As Williams starts to hoist himself in there is the sharp explosion of a rifle above the pounding of the machine gun, and Williams is knocked off his feet by the impact in his left arm. White turns aft, in the direction of the shot, as Weinberg springs down and helps Williams get to his feet and into the plane, others inside reaching out and helping.

384. MED. LONG SHOT AFT
The one running Jap is racing toward camera with lowered bayonet. He has nearly reached the tail and is out of range of Winocki's machine gun.

385. CLOSE SHOT WHITE
as he whips his spanner with a beautiful hard throw at

386. JAP
as he runs into camera and the spanner catches him square in the face and he goes down like a shot rabbit.

387. INT. DOOR SECTION OF MARY ANN

Weinberg and Winocki in one swift movement haul White into the ship and slam the door as the engines roar and the airplane rolls forward.

388. INT. COCKPIT CLOSE ON TEX RADER

as he shoves the throttles wide open and peers ahead, trying to clear the trees that hedge in this clearing.

389. LONG SHOT MARY ANN

She rolls faster, her great engines roaring, as she just clears the trees at the edge of the field and then gathers speed as she reaches the runway.

LAP DISSOLVE:

390. LONG SHOT MARY ANN

She comes roaring toward the end of the field and lifts into the graying sky of breaking day—safe.

391. INT. COCKPIT CLOSE ON TEX

straining every nerve, immense relief on his face. Sergeant White enters with Williams, whose left arm hangs limp at his side. But Williams is grinning, and as Tex looks around anxiously he slaps Tex on the back and slides down into his own seat as we

FADE OUT

FADE IN

392. LONG SHOT MARY ANN (FROM CAMERA PLANE) DAY

flying high above unbroken clouds.

LAP:

392A. INSERT CHART

Hauser's pencil draws a thin line from Manila, across the Celebes Sea, to Port Darwin, Australia. Then it marks the airplane's position with a small circle on the line, at about 4 degrees north and 124 degrees 30 minutes east.

392B. INT. MEAT CAN CLOSE SHOT HAUSER
working over his chart as White crawls down through the hatch behind him and comes to the chart table.

WHITE:
How we doing, sir?

HAUSER:
For a plane they said wouldn't ever fly again, I think we're doing fine, chief. How's our fuel consumption?

WHITE:
Nothing to worry about. We'll make Australia all right— (Grins.) that is, if you can find it, sir.

HAUSER (smiles):
Can't very well miss it, can we? This is a navigator's holiday. (Then soberly.) How's Lieutenant Williams?

WHITE (proudly):
Didn't even wince when I set his arm, sir. He had about two hours' sleep and now you can't pry him outa that copilot's seat.

392C. INT. COCKPIT
Tex Rader flying the ship. Williams, in copilot's seat, has his left arm crudely splinted and trussed to his chest. Outside of that he seems little the worse for wear. Tommy McMartin enters from catwalk and leans behind them.

McMARTIN:
Arm hurting, Bill?

WILLIAMS:
It's okay. How's the crew?

McMARTIN:
They're only worried about leaving the war behind us.

WILLIAMS:

It'll catch up with us. Peterson just picked up some news on the radio.

McMARTIN:

How's that?

WILLIAMS:

Big Jap invasion fleet headed for Australia. That's what they think, anyway. Our Pacific Fleet is out hunting it.

McMARTIN (peers down through window at the floor of clouds):

Well, I wish 'em luck. Me, I haven't seen anything but clouds since daylight.

WILLIAMS:

I hope we have time to fix up *Mary Ann* before the Jap hits Australia.

TEX:

All I hope is that they've got some P-40s in Darwin. If they haven't, I'm going to resign from the Air Corps and take up knitting.

WILLIAMS (glares at Tex, then to Tommy):

I think he's the guy that shot me in the arm—just so he could get in that seat.

TEX (grins):

Don't do me an injustice, Bill. I'd only shoot you to get out of this seat.

Williams looks at McMartin eloquently and Tommy shrugs and shakes his head as if Tex were a hopeless case.

392D. INT. RADIO SECTION

Peterson at radio. Weinberg and Callahan are sitting on the floor playing with the little dog, Tripoli. Winocki leans in the doorway watching them. Then Winocki glances over his shoulder along catwalk and sees White coming. Signals to the two quickly.

WINOCKI:
Here he comes.

Quickly Weinberg and Callahan grab Tripoli and stuff him back in a corner behind some parachutes, an instant before White enters, Winocki making room for him. White looks around and observes their studied nonchalance. It puzzles him.

PETERSON (to distract his attention):
Say, Sergeant, do they grow apples in Australia?

WHITE (suspiciously, watching the others):
Don't you guys never sleep?

WEINBERG:
We kinda got outa the habit, chief.

Then White's face reacts as he sees:

392E. VERY CLOSE SHOT
the little dog peeking out from behind a parachute in the corner.

392F. CLOSE GROUP SHOT
White points indignantly.

WHITE:
So *that's* what you been hiding. I knew there was something.

WINOCKI (dryly):
Well, you said to give him to the marines.

CALLAHAN:
He follered me right into this airplane, Sergeant.

WHITE (gruffly):
Well, you don't need to make a mystery about it. Don't you suppose I like dogs?

Tripoli crawls out and White stoops down to him as the others look at each other wonderingly, and Weinberg (behind White's back) makes a "how could I know" gesture with uplifted hands.

392G. INT. MEAT CAN CLOSE SHOT HAUSER
in the Plexiglas nose as he lifts his octant to take a sun shot. As he lowers it he happens to glance down and reacts at sight of:

392H. DOWNWARD SHOT
a solid floor of cloud, but through a break we glimpse a tiny fleet far below.

392I. CLOSE SHOT HAUSER
for reaction. Then he puts down his octant, jerks on headphones as he calls excitedly.

HAUSER:
Navigator to pilot!

392J. INT. COCKPIT
Tex switches on interphone.

TEX:
Go ahead, Monk.

HAUSER'S VOICE:
Look down below!

Both Tex and Williams peer down through windows.

TEX:
I don't see anything.

HAUSER'S VOICE:
Right under us! Bank her a bit!

Tex moves the controls and the ship banks over. Williams rises from his seat to peer down through the side window.

392K. SHOT THROUGH WINDOW
The break is larger now and we can see the whole fleet spread out.

392L. CLOSE INTO FACES OF TEX AND WILLIAMS
for reaction.

WILLIAMS:
That must be our fleet—looking for the Japs.

At that instant there is a *kerpoom* and we see the explosion of a shell a hundred yards away, through the window, and feel the shock of the explosion. Instantly Tex rights the ship and climbs for altitude. White comes plunging in from catwalk and grips the chair backs.

WHITE:
Japs, sir?

Tex nods as he switches on interphone.

TEX:
Get the crew to their stations!

392M. INT. MEAT CAN
Hauser bent over in the glass nose looking below. Shooting down past his head we glimpse the fleet, and then the cloud break closes and they are invisible as McMartin comes crawling in swiftly.

TEX'S VOICE:
Pilot to navigator!

HAUSER:
Go ahead.

TEX'S VOICE:
Looks like we drew the jackpot. Have you got our position?

HAUSER:
I was just checking it. Three fifty north, one twenty-four thirty east.

McMARTIN (pulls on headphones):
Bombardier to pilot! Give me a crack at 'em, Tex!

392N. INT. COCKPIT TEX AND WILLIAMS
very tense as another shell bursts some distance away.

TEX (on interphone):
Shut up and sit tight, Tommy. We're gonna start a war, not a fight . . . Pilot to radio!

392O. INT. RADIO SECTION WEINBERG, CALLAHAN, AND WINOCKI
gathered tensely around Peterson as White enters hurriedly along catwalk.

PETERSON:
Go ahead, sir.

TEX'S VOICE:
Write down this position—three fifty north, one twenty-four thirty east. Got it?

PETERSON:
Yes, sir. Three fifty north, one twenty-four thirty east.

TEX'S VOICE:
Broadcast it to our carriers, to the Army Air Corps, to everyone you can reach. Tell 'em Jap task force sighted, headed south, that position. Got it?

PETERSON:
Yes, sir.

TEX'S VOICE:
Hop to it. Burn up that radio. We're going upstairs and play hide-and-seek till we get reinforcements.

Peterson throws a switch and begins to send rapidly with his key as White motions the others.

WHITE:

Weinberg. You and Callahan get on those waist guns. Winocki. Now you're gonna get a chance to try that fancy tail gun you rigged up. Come on, let's show 'em what that Star-Spangled Banner can do when it gets mad!

The three pile aft as White climbs into the top turret. Peterson is working his key in a fury. (Now we hear the singing sound of dots and dashes, and they carry over ensuing cuts like an alarm.)

392P. INSERT PETERSON'S HAND
working the transmitting key.

392Q. UPWARD SHOT AN ARMY RADIO TOWER ON LAND

392R. INT. RADIO ROOM CLOSE SHOT ARMY RADIO OPERATOR
as he writes swiftly, tears sheet from pad, and hands it to an Air Corps major who exits swiftly with it.

392S. ANOTHER RADIO TOWER AT DIFFERENT ANGLE

392T. INT. TENT CLOSE SHOT ARMY RADIOMAN
as he jerks sheet from typewriter and hands it to an orderly who runs out with it.

392U. INSERT PETERSON'S HAND
working key.

392V. INT. RADIO ROOM ON SHIPBOARD
A navy operator writes swiftly, tears off form, and hands it to second operator, who buzzes phone, to read it.

392W. BRIDGE OF AIRCRAFT CARRIER
(just an impression of a corner of it). Naval officer on telephone as the message is read.

392X. LONG SHOT AMERICAN CARRIER
Planes taking off.

392Y. INSERT PETERSON'S HAND
working key.

392Z. UPWARD ANGLE ON AERIAL WIRES
of another American carrier.

392AA. DECK OF CARRIER
A rating dashes along deck and hands form to an officer.

392BB. LONG SHOT SECOND CARRIER
as planes are taking off.

392CC. LONG SHOT SECOND CARRIER
as planes are taking off.

393. INSERT PETERSON'S HAND
sending.

393A. DECK OF CARRIER
Naval torpedo planes taking off.

393B. ARMY AIR CORPS RADIO TOWER

393C. AIRFIELD SHOTS OF B-17S
taking off, one after another.[7]

393D. MED. LONG FLYING SHOT OF MARY ANN (MINIATURE)
She is hardly visible, flying blind in the cloud.

393E. INSERT PETERSON'S HAND
as it works the key, acknowledging a message. Camera pulls back swiftly as Peterson, now alone in the compartment (we can see only the legs of White who stands in top turret), switches to interphone. (Vapor masks window.)

PETERSON:
Operator to pilot.

TEX'S VOICE:
Go ahead.

PETERSON:
Group of Army bombers and Navy torpedo planes have reached approximate position, sir. They want you to go down and lead 'em in. Formation leader's calling you on command set.

393F. INT. COCKPIT CLOSE ON TEX AND WILLIAMS
Thick vapor outside windows.

TEX (on interphone):
Okay, Peterson. Good work. Get to your turret.

393G. INT. RADIO SECTION

PETERSON:
Yes, sir. (Unjacks his headphones and starts crawling into bottom turret.)

393H. INT. COCKPIT
Tex calls on interphone as he noses down.

TEX:
Here we go, fellows. Watch the fireworks. (Switches to command set.) Zero five five six four to all airplanes. Zero five five six four to all airplanes—

LAP DISSOLVE TO:

394–407. OMITTED (INCLUDED IN FOREGOING)

408. FULL SHOT JAPANESE FLEET
Destroyers are putting on speed and belching smoke. Cruisers turn to protect a big carrier, laying smoke screens. Antiaircraft guns begin to spurt flame.

409. CLOSE SHOT JAPANESE FLAG
whipping from the mast of the flagship. Pan down to Japanese admiral and staff on the bridge. They are looking up at:

410. SKY SHOT MARY ANN
nosing down through cloud toward fleet, shells bursting around her.

411. BRIDGE OF FLAGSHIP
A staff officer points off at

412. LONG SHOT HUGE FLIGHT OF B-17S
approaching from another direction.

413. BRIDGE OF FLAGSHIP
Some of the officers run aft as the admiral turns and looks another direction at

414. LONG SHOT FLIGHT OF B-25S
coming in toward the fleet.

415. FULL SHOT FLEET
Now the ships all begin to change formation, laying thick smoke screen everywhere and the AA fire is terrific.

416. MED. LONG SHOT MARY ANN
from camera plane. Shell bursts beyond her. Bomb bay doors opening.

417. INT. COCKPIT TEX AND WILLIAMS
Shell bursts visible through windows and we hear their explosions.

TEX (on interphone):
Get ready for your run, Tommy. How d'you want it?

418. INT. MEAT CAN CLOSE SHOT McMARTIN
frozen over his bombsight.

McMARTIN:
Take 'em in line and I'll pour 'em down their funnels.

TEX'S VOICE:
Don't waste any eggs, Popeye.

McMARTIN:
You watch the basket, I'll lay the eggs.

TEX'S VOICE:
She's all yours. Speed three one five.

McMARTIN:
Three one five—check!

419. SHOOTING DOWN PAST HIS CROUCHED BODY
we see the Japanese fleet spread out more than a mile below, AA guns spurting fire.

420. FLASH CLOSE-UP WHITE
in the top turret waiting. Shell bursts outside.

421. FLASH CLOSE-UP PETERSON
in bottom turret. Through the glass cage we glimpse the fleet below.

422. INT. WAIST SECTION FLASH CLOSE SHOT WEINBERG
at one gun, Callahan at the other.

423. INT. TAIL FLASH CLOSE-UP WINOCKI
lying on his belly over his machine gun, which sticks out the open end of the sawed-off tail.

424. NEAR SHOT MARY ANN
as bombs begin to spill out of her open bomb bays. (NOTE: Following from miniature stuff already shot or shooting.)

425. FULL SHOT GROUP OF JAPANESE SHIPS
featuring a tanker. They are blasted by the falling bombs.

426. FLASH DECK OF TANKER
Twenty men in a breakaway explosion.

427. DECK OF TANKER
A sheet of flame envelops men.

428. DECK OF TANKER
Jap sailors firing AA guns.

429. WATERLINE SHOT ON TANKER
Japs fall into the water and burning oil pours across them.

430. LONG SHOT MARY ANN
Shells bursting around her. Half a dozen Jap Zeros are coming down after her.

431. NEAR SHOT MARY ANN
More bombs spill from her open bays.

432. INT. MEAT CAN SHOOTING DOWN PAST McMARTIN'S HEAD
We see the bombs hit warship far below, water and black smoke belching up.

McMARTIN (yells on interphone):
Another bull's-eye!

433. INT. COCKPIT
Tex yells on interphone.

TEX:
I don't believe it. You can't be that good.

McMARTIN'S VOICE:
Wait till you make your turn and see for yourself.

434. NEAR SHOT MARY ANN
as more bombs spill from her belly.

435. FULL SHOT GROUP OF JAP TRANSPORTS
Destroyers are dashing past to lay smoke screens. Bombs rain down in a succession of terrible explosions. Destroyers are driven off. Transport launches rafts but sinks.

436. TORPEDO PLANE
drops torpedo and screams on just over the masts of the Jap battleship. We see the torpedo explode against the hull of the battleship, whose AA guns are still firing. Airplanes crash through smoke into the sea.

437. BRIDGE OF JAP BATTLESHIP
Officers and men. A direct hit by a bomb.

438. NEAR SHOT OF THE MAST
as it topples, carrying the Japanese flag through black smoke into the sea as it falls.

439. FULL SHOT JAP CARRIER AND GROUP OF PROTECTING SHIPS
Bombs hit the carrier, near misses heaving up great fountains of water. Destroyers come steaming in and stand by. The carrier turns and lists. There is a tremendous gasoline explosion and some of her planes are thrown off into the sea.

440. NEAR SHOT MARY ANN
Her machine guns firing in bursts as she heads into the thick of the dogfight. Another stick of bombs falls from her bays.

441. FULL SHOT JAP CONVOY
Carrier and destroyers standing by. The carrier is burning fiercely. Carrier and destroyers hit by bombs from

Mary Ann. A bomb goes down the stack of a destroyer, there is a violent explosion, and the destroyer rams the carrier. There is a terrific powder magazine explosion and the ships are blown up.

442. NEAR SHOT MARY ANN
Her guns blasting as bomb bay doors start to close.

443. INT. BOMB BAY SHOT DOWN THROUGH EMPTY RACKS
and closing doors. We glimpse the burning, smoking, sinking Japanese force a mile below.

444. INT. MEAT CAN
McMartin sings out on interphone.

McMARTIN:
Bombs all away!

There is a thud and explosion, and he almost spills from his chair as the ship lurches and staggers.

445. CLOSE SHOT LEADING EDGE OF WING MINIATURE
We see number three engine, torn from its nacelle by a shell, fall from the plane.

446. INT. COCKPIT CLOSE ON TEX AND WILLIAMS
as Tex fights to control the weaving ship and Williams nurses the throttles, trying to balance the three remaining engines.

447. INT. WAIST CLOSE ON WEINBERG AND CALLAHAN
back to back at their guns. The ship is lurching and groaning, and Callahan nudges Weinberg anxiously.

CALLAHAN (shouts):
Anything wrong?

WEINBERG (grins, glued to his gun):
She always does dis when she's mad! (Cuts loose with his gun.)

Now the din of destruction, both in the sky and on the sea, is so terrific that we cannot distinguish one gun above another.

448. LONG SHOT MARY ANN
A flock of Zeros comes roaring down at her.

449. NEAR SHOT MARY ANN
Her guns all blasting at the Zeros.

450. INT. COCKPIT CLOSE SHOT TEX AND WILLIAMS
Then machine guns pound and bullets rip through the windows and Tex swiftly maneuvers.

451. LONG SHOT MARY ANN
Jap Zeros peel off and dive for her tail.

452. CLOSE SHOT TIP TURRET
White swings his gun up and cuts loose.

453. INT. WAIST SECTION
Hauser and Callahan are firing at the oncoming Zeros.

454. INT. COCKPIT
Williams switches on interphone as he yells above the pounding guns.

WILLIAMS:

Wait for 'em, Winocki! They don't know we got a stinger in our tail!

455. TAIL CLOSE SHOT INTO WINOCKI'S FACE
as he waits with his machine gun in the sawed-off tail. We hear the machine guns of the Japs. Then Winocki cuts loose.

456. FLASH OF JAP ZERO
as it disintegrates in black smoke.

457. CLOSE SHOT WINOCKI
He waits a moment and then cuts loose again.

458. SHOT OF ANOTHER JAP PLANE
going to pieces in the close blast.

459. CLOSE SHOT WINOCKI
as he yells on interphone.

WINOCKI:
They're comin' in like fool chickens for more corn! (Cuts loose again.)

460. FLASH OF A THIRD ZERO
as it disintegrates.

461. EXT. TAIL CLOSE SHOT
We see bullets rip through the metal.

462. INT. TAIL CLOSE SHOT WINOCKI
as he is hit and collapses over his gun.

463. NEAR SHOT MARY ANN
with one wing tip close to camera. Bullets rip through the wing tip and several plates fly off. The ship wobbles dangerously.

464. INT. WAIST SECTION
Weinberg and Callahan back to back at their guns. Callahan stops firing to peer out window at:

465. WING TIP FROM HIS ANGLE
A couple of more plates are whipped off by the blast of air and fly past window.

466. CLOSE SHOT CALLAHAN
as he yells on interphone.

CALLAHAN:

Hey, Captain—that wing's comin' off!

467. INT. COCKPIT

Williams too is watching that wing anxiously as Tex yells on interphone with a wild grin.

TEX:

Don't worry, Callahan—this crate will fly on one wing!

468. INT. WAIST SECTION

Callahan takes a reassured look at the disintegrating wing and yells over his shoulder to Weinberg.

CALLAHAN:

Nothin' to worry about, Weinberg! She's okay!

Then bullets rip through the fuselage from Zeros and Weinberg cuts loose with a burst. He yells at the top of his voice—the first time we have seen him really mad.

WEINBERG:

Come on, youse! Come closer an' I'll fight youse wit me fists! (Cuts loose again but bullets rip through the window and he goes down. Tries to get up to his gun again but cannot. Callahan turns to help him but he yells angrily.) *Keep on shootin'!*

469. CLOSE SHOT NUMBER TWO ENGINE

Bullets hit it and it stops.

470. INT. COCKPIT CLOSE ON TEX AND WILLIAMS

as White comes plunging in behind them, motioning off at the wing. Ship is beginning to rock and stagger. (Fast tempo for dialogue.)

WHITE (yells hoarsely):

She's goin' to pieces, sir!

WILLIAMS (to Tex):

Looks like we got to blow taps! Pull out! Head south! (Snaps on interphone.) Monk! Dig for land, Monk! Give us a course! I'll settle for an island four feet wide! (Yells to Tex.) Keep her nose up, Tex! I still believe in miracles!

TEX (fighting controls and trying to steady the shuddering ship):

Boy, this is *it*.

WILLIAMS (over shoulder to Robbie):

Look after the crew, chief! (As chief starts aft.) AND KEEP THOSE TWO ENGINES TURNING!

WHITE (yells back):

Yes, *sir*.

WILLIAMS (snaps on radio):

Zero five five six four to group leader—zero five five six four to group leader! Sorry to leave this shindig, sir, but we're goin' down for repairs! Kiss the boys goodbye and GOD BLESS AMERICA! (Yells to Tex.) Ease 'er, ease 'er, Tex! Keep her chin up!

TEX (grimly fighting ship):

You worry about your own chin, miracle man![8]

470A. LONG SHOT OF MARY ANN

leaving formation or pick up some sort of shot. You could go into group leader's plane and see the crippled *Mary Ann* through window and show the group leader lifting his hand in silent farewell, just as the guns begin to bark aft.

471. AUSTRALIA A LONELY BEACH NIGHT

Shooting out across the moonlight sea we see nothing at first, but hear the uneven throbbing of two airplane engines. As the sound grows louder we can make out the shape of a big airplane swinging in toward the beach, almost touching the water. As she swings in closer she clips a wave or two and then as she tries to lift, another motor cuts off and she slams up on the flat sand with a grinding roar, rises half up on her nose, and settles back again. Flames spurt up from one of her engines.[9]

472. NEAR SHOT OF THE WRECKED PLANE
The flames grow rapidly at the front edge as the door is flung open and two men start dragging others out of the airplane.

473. CLOSER SHOT AT DOORWAY
We see the two unwounded men are Sergeant White and Tex. The crackling flames illuminate them brightly now and they work in swift and unspeaking desperation. Tex grabs hold of the men as White lowers them out. Winocki is half conscious but able to stand dazedly. Hauser is so weak he can hardly stand but totters away from the burning ship. Williams, his arm still trussed up, insists on trying to help get the others out. Weinberg is lowered painfully and crawls away on the sand. Callahan has his eyes and face bandaged and has to be led away. Tommy McMartin climbs out but seems in a daze, his face streaked with blood. Then the little dog, Tripoli, jumps out by himself, quite unharmed. Finally they lift out Peterson, and White jumps down feverishly, and in the increasing glare of the burning plane they walk, crawl, lift, and carry the whole crew.

SLOW DISSOLVE TO:

474. INT. SQUADRON ORDERLY ROOM FULL SHOT NIGHT
Outside the window there is a flagpole and an American flag. About thirty fine-looking lads, all of them in their early twenties—fine, eager, fresh-looking faces—grouped around a colonel (Stanley Ridges) who is giving them last minute instructions. The room is rather long and narrow. Through windows we can see palm trees silhouetted against the twilight sky. We are at a

landing field somewhere in the Pacific within good striking distance of Japan. At the moment it is Guadalcanal in the Solomons; next month it may be somewhere else; we do not specify. As we dissolve in, we have no notion of where we are, keeping it in suspense. It is only through the quiet words of the colonel that we will find out. The scene should bring to mind the opening scene of our story, when preparations were for a routine flight in peacetime, except that the officers are all much younger, excepting the colonel. (In this shot the officers from the *Mary Ann* have their backs to camera or out of frame, and we keep their final fate in suspense until we wish to pan to them or reverse on their faces or bring them in with camera movement.)

The colonel has maps on the table at center of group. During his quiet talk he may bend over it to indicate something, light a cigarette, or walk up and down. It is very quiet and man-to-man, avoiding any sense of heroics. No one of the listening lads moves.

COLONEL:

Well, fellows, this is it. This is what we've been waiting for. I've only got one regret—that I'm not included in this party. They say I'm getting a little old . . . Of course, that's a lie, but if you don't tell anybody I'll own up that any one of you young fellows could fly rings around me—outfly me—and outshoot me. Probably outguess me, too. You've got good planes—the best of their kind in the world. And you know how to handle 'em—you've flown 'em halfway around the world to get here. You're a long way from home. But if you look at it another way, this is home too. (Looks around at them.) A month ago the Jap meatball hung out there on that flagpole. Now that's our flag planted out there. Now this is American soil—and we've got another base where we can hit the enemy—and hit 'em hard. We've been waiting for this a long time. (Walks.) I wish I could tell you about the first days of the war. We took an awful beating—there weren't very many of us then—but now it's different. (Looks them over.) There's hundreds more like you on their way here—and thousands more training. And there's a million-man Air Force behind you fellows. As far as that goes there's a hundred and thirty million of our folks back home behind the Air Force. (Pauses, remembering.) Yep, we took our beating—took it for a long time. A lot of good men died—but those who got through learned a lot. Every man who came through those bad days is worth a lot now because each of them can get you new fellows through the one thing you lack—one thing you can't get in training—and that's combat experience. When you get back here tomorrow—and you'll get back, all of you—you'll know what I mean. (Quietly, with a change of tone.) Tonight your target is Tokyo—and you're going to play the "Star-Spangled Banner" with two-ton bombs! All you've got to do is remember what you've learned and follow your squadron leaders.

Now the camera shows at whom the boys are looking almost with veneration: Rader, Williams, McMartin, and Hauser. Play following lines over their faces.

COLONEL (continuing):

Williams will lead the first section, Rader the second. Hauser is navigating for the squadron, and McMartin will talk to you bombardiers before taking off. (While he is speaking, camera pulls back to a full shot.) Well, that's all. Good luck to you—and give 'em hell.[10]

DISSOLVE TO:

475. EXT. FIELD WIDE ANGLE

on one of the big airplanes, twilight effect. (Match lighting of takeoff from Mather Field.) Crew gathered around near door. Winocki, Weinberg, Peterson, White. McMartin and Hauser climbing in. A very young kid, even younger than Chester, is shyly waiting with Robbie as Williams comes striding out to plane. Camera moves in or cuts closer.

WILLIAMS:

Everything ready, Robbie?

WHITE (just as at opening of story):

Yes, sir. (Indicates new kid who moves in admiringly, a little awed by Williams.) This is our new gunner, Captain. Private Wilson—replacing Chester at second radio.

WILLIAMS (with old manner of Quincannon, kindly):

Glad to have you with us, Wilson.

KID (with Chester's manner, eagerly):

I'm glad to be with you, sir.

He steps past kid to the door with Robbie. Camera moves in or cuts close to take in the name *Mary Ann* from the old ship. Williams, about to swing in, looks at it and then at Robbie's face, and White's expression shows that he planned this as a surprise, very pleased with himself.

WILLIAMS:

Seems like we've done this before, Robbie.

WHITE:

Not like this, sir.

WILLIAMS:

No. I guess you're right.

He pats the name and climbs in, followed by White. The balance of the crew follows.

CUT TO:

476. INT. COCKPIT CLOSE ON A YOUNG COPILOT whom we saw in room during colonel's talk. He is already seated as Williams enters and slides into pilot's seat followed by Robbie. Williams begins checking over things and then notes what we do—the young fellow hanging something from the hook beside him.

WILLIAMS:
What's that, Jimmy?

Copilot shyly shows what it is—a small rag doll.

COPILOT:
Just for luck, skipper. My kid gave it to me.

Williams looks strangely at Robbie, who looks back at him just as strangely, hearing the echo of Quincannon.

WILLIAMS:
All set, Robbie?

WHITE:
Yes, sir.

WILLIAMS:
Okay, we'll start 'em up.

Begins starting engines. The "Battle Hymn of the Republic," which we have heard from the commencement of the tag, almost inaudibly over colonel's talk, grows louder.

CUT TO:

477. INT. PLANE RADIO SECTION Camera pulls back or pans to take in the new kid with Weinberg, Winocki, and Peterson. The kid looks at the ship with awed admiration, a glow of pride in his face.

KID:
Gee, we're lucky. I bet there's a million fellows back home would like to be in my shoes!

Weinberg and Winocki look strangely at each other, hearing the echo of Chester. But there is no mockery in their faces this time.

WINOCKI:

Yeah, you're right, kid.

WEINBERG (grins):

Sure t'ing, an' we're gonna see you get back home to tell 'em about it.

DISSOLVE TO:

478. SHOTS OF TAKEOFF

The "Battle Hymn" swells up, louder and louder.

479. BEAUTIFUL SHOT OF THE NINE FORTRESSES IN FORMATION OVER THE SEA

Now the "Battle Hymn" swells triumphantly until it thunders with a sense of victory, as we

FADE OUT

THE END

Notes to the Screenplay

As noted in the Introduction, the dialogue contained in the Revised Final shooting script dated July 3 to October 8, 1942, bears only a general relationship to the dialogue spoken by the characters in the film. On the other hand, except for the following differences, the Revised Final script does tell the exact story that is visually portrayed in the film.

1 Scenes 42–44 introduce Lieutenant Rader as Lieutenant Williams's rival during the flight from San Francisco to Hawaii. In the film, there is no indication that Williams has competition until Susan mentions Rader in the hospital sequence.

2 Although in the screenplay Winocki admits to Weinberg that he went to Notre Dame so that he could get into flying school, in the film there is no mention of Winocki's education or long-standing desire to be a pilot. In fact, Garfield plays the character as a rough, unsophisticated man, not a college graduate.

3 In the film, Quincannon describes the death of White's son in words, not just actions.

4 In the film, the action goes from Hauser's saying, "We're thirty miles off the coast," in scene 230, to scene 254, after which White spots the Japanese fighters and the aerial combat begins. The *Mary Ann* drops no bombs until the final battle. Some of the interior action described in the script in the missing scenes, including White's reaction to his son's death (scene 251), does appear in the film, but there are no shots of the Japanese fleet.

The deletion of the combat sequences, taken from the miniature work, was accomplished simply by cutting from the *Mary Ann* as it flies through the clouds to a shot of Japanese planes swooping down on the bomber. The scenes were undoubtedly cut from the film because of its length and redundancy with the final battle. To have included them would have reduced the dramatic impact of ending the film with one major battle.

5 Although the script describes the aerial battle (scenes 258–75B) without dialogue, Hawks apparently improvised some with the help of Triffy. In the film, however, there is no radio conversation between Quincannon and Rader as in scene 275A.

6 In the movie, Winocki belly-lands the plane because he cannot get the gear down.

7 Scenes 392A to 393C describe the armada of planes taking off to attack the Japanese fleet. As noted in the Introduction, the U.S. Navy had no carriers and the Air Force had no large numbers of bombers anywhere near the Philippines in the first weeks of the war when *Air Force* purports to take place.

8 Scenes 408 to 470 describing the climactic battle served only as a framework to help Hawks to film the crew in action and the editors to put together the montage. The actual dialogue is much sparser than in the script. And, in the film, Winocki is not wounded (scene 462).

9 Scene 471 has the *Mary Ann* crash-land on an Australian beach; in the film, the plane lands in the surf. The footage looks genuine rather than staged with a miniature and could well be a piece of combat film—the waves breaking on the beach look real whereas water used in miniature work invariably lacks visual authenticity.

10 Although the script gives a detailed description of the briefing, the film limits itself to a short preflight briefing and ends with a montage of B-17s taking off into the dusk with a voice-over of President Roosevelt's Declaration of War speech.

The problem of creating an ending grew out of the reality that the dramatic climax to *Air Force* came with the destruction of the Japanese fleet. But Hawks had to get the crew of the *Mary Ann* safely on the ground. Then, since the film needed an upbeat message ending, the director had to add the promise of the first heavy bomber attack on Japan. So, the crew of the *Mary Ann* are brought together. Williams has become the leader of the first section and Rader, now a confirmed bomber pilot, of the second. Hauser has become navigator of the whole squadron and McMartin is the lead bombardier.

Production Credits

Produced by	Hal B. Wallis
Directed by	Howard Hawks
Screenplay by	Dudley Nichols
Director of Photography	James Wong Howe
Aerial Photography by	Elmer Dyer and Charles Marshall
Film Editor	George Amy
Art Director	John Hughes
Chief Pilot for Warner Brothers	Paul Mantz
Special Effects by	Roy Davidson Rex Wimpy H. F. Koenekamp
Sound by	Oliver S. Garretson
Gowns by	Milo Anderson
Makeup by	Perc Westmore
Set Decorations by	Walter F. Tilford
Music by	Franz Waxman
Music Director	Leo F. Forbstein

Released: February 1943
Running time: 124 minutes

Cast

Captain Michael Quincannon	John Ridgely
Lieutenant Bill Williams	Gig Young
Lieutenant Tommy McMartin	Arthur Kennedy
Lieutenant Monk Hauser	Charles Drake
Sergeant Robbie White	Harry Carey
Corporal B. B. Weinberg	George Tobias
Corporal Gus Peterson	Ward Wood
Private Henry Chester	Ray Montgomery
Sergeant Joe Winocki	John Garfield
Lieutenant Tex Rader	James Brown
Major Mallory	Stanley Ridges
Colonel Blake	Moroni Olsen
A Colonel	Willard Robertson
Sergeant Callahan	Edward S. Brophy
Major Roberts	Richard Lane
Lieutenant Moran	Bill Crago
Susan McMartin	Faye Emerson
Major Daniels	Addison Richards
Major Bagley	James Flavin
Mary Quincannon	Ann Doran
Mrs. Chester	Dorothy Peterson

Inventory

The following materials from the Warner library of the Wisconsin Center for Film and Theater Research were used by Suid in preparing *Air Force* for the Wisconsin/Warner Bros. Screenplay Series:

Temporary, by Dudley Nichols. April 24, 1942. Incomplete. 193 pages.
Revised Temporary, no author shown. May 29, 1942. 189 pages.
Second Revised Temporary, no author shown. June 12 to June 13, 1942. 207 pages.
Final, no author shown. June 18 to June 30, 1942. Incomplete. 140 pages.
Revised Final, by Nichols. July 3 with revisions to October 8, 1942. 184 pages.